Remember the Good Times

David H. Smith

Broadman Press
Nashville, Tennessee

Dewey Decimal Classification: 253.2
Subject heading: MINISTERS' CHILDREN

Library of Congress Catalog Card Number: 78–066817
Printed in the United States of America.

Contents

I. Getting Acquainted

My first memories are of attending church services. I'm not sure how old I was, but thankfully I was young enough to be permitted to carry a small pillow with me. That little headrest caused a lot of comment. Some members reminded me of that cushion long after it had been discarded.

Of course I had to sit and sleep on the front seat. Mother played the piano, Dad preached, and there was no way I could avoid constant scrutiny. The evening services were especially difficult. I'm afraid I went to sleep rather early most of the time.

One pleasant memory is of learning to place a forefinger in my ear. This wasn't done to block the sound but to enhance the congregational singing. A properly placed finger that is moved back and forth to the beat of the music adds a new dimension to most hymns. The only problem was that some second-seat singers snickered when they saw me do this. Dad never approved of my attempts to improve the sound of First Baptist's singing.

I have another early memory. It is of Mother being ill, Dad being very sad, and of going to a cemetery. Two men went with Dad and me. We took a small coffin with us. One of the men prayed, then Dad and I left. He explained as best he could that my new little brother could only stay with us for a few hours before he had to go see Jesus.

About ten years later, after greeting three lovely little sisters, I said hello to a real, live baby brother. By then it was evident he would need some written instructions if he were to make it as a PK.

Memo 1: Hello, Little PK

You got born today, and you look awful little and squirmy. You look awful skinny and kind of red and wrinkled too. Since you're little and your daddy is a preacher, I think you are going to have a hard time getting along. So I'm going to start right now to write down some things to help you since I'm almost a teenager and you are my little brother.

You have three sisters older than you. They are kind of different. They pick at their food, comb their hair, wash a lot, and don't want to wait until I'm through with the funny paper before they read it. When they do read the paper they cut out the people for paper dolls and then nobody can read it. Sometimes, when Dad has to go someplace Sunday afternoon, they cut up the paper before he reads it and then there is real trouble!

I knew you were coming. Mamma had been getting fatter. Somebody told me you could tell before babies were born that they were going to get born 'cause their mothers got fat. I've checked this out a few times and it is true. You watch and see for yourself when you get a little bigger.

There were some other things that gave me an idea you were coming. The ladies began giving Mom a lot of white rags. She washed them and heated them in the oven and then folded them up to put away. I asked her about all the rags.

"You never know when you may need cloth for bandages. You may stump your toe someday and want me to put turpentine on it and wrap it up," she said. That threw me off for a few days. Then I figured, *I don't stump my toe enough to use up all those rags.*

Yesterday morning we all had to get dressed up and go to our pastor's house. I wondered why we had to go up there in the morning. Sunday School meetings are in the afternoon and at night. Class parties are at night, but the preacher's wife isn't my teacher. When I asked why we were going up there, Daddy told me, "You haven't visited the preacher's house in quite a spell. He'd probably like to see all of you some day other than Sunday."

Now that didn't make sense 'cause the preacher's house is only up the street two blocks. Dad must have noticed the look on my face because he said, "Now you stay up there and help look after Brother Sisk's two boys until he tells you it's time to come home. And you help Mrs. Sisk look after your sisters."

If it sounds funny for us to go to our preacher's house when Dad is a preacher, it's because Dad doesn't preach at our church.

He's a missionary in our association, which is why he's mostly gone on Sunday when the paper comes and doesn't get back sometimes until after it's all cut up by the girls. But I told you about that before. But it's important. When you can't play ball or shinny on Sunday because your Dad's a preacher, the paper is important.

Anyway, we all got dressed. Dad didn't do a very good job cooking the oats for breakfast that morning. They were runny. Either he put in too much water or maybe we were about out of oats again. The milk was runny too. He put too much water for the powder or he didn't stir it enough and it all settled on the bottom of the big pitcher. It had been like this a lot since Mom didn't feel good enough to cook in the mornings.

I led the girls up the street past the school superintendent's house. He's the principal's boss. We didn't make any noise when we went by his place. His kids make as big a racket as everybody's kids, but he doesn't do anything about what they do. He just picks on other kids.

We went down the street across from the ball diamond. I was glad nobody was playing because I would have wanted the girls to go on by themselves while I played a game or two. This probably would have caused some trouble.

Then we went by the doctor's house. He has a car and a big house. His boy has a car too. His boy is the principal where I used to go to school. He takes me to the fairgrounds and hits golf balls out in the middle of the racetrack. I shag them until my pockets are full then take them back to him. He usually gives me a dollar. I have to run a lot and it gets pretty tiresome, but that's a lot of money just for chasing golf balls. He is pretty nice to me. I don't know whether it's because he saw Dad have to pay a lot for schoolbooks or because I saw him kissing the teacher down in the school basement.

We moved to town just before the start of school so all the used books had been sold or traded. We had to buy mostly new books and they cost an awful lot. Dad was white-faced when he counted up the bill, but he said, "There's nothing I can do but take them."

The principal was in the book store, and he talked to the manager and then he took back a book or two. After school started I found those books in my desk.

I figured the principal got them for me. He didn't say anything and I figured if he wanted it that way I wouldn't mention it either. So that's why when I was bilious one day and down in the nurse's room when he kissed the teacher, I didn't say anything.

When he came down I thought it was to see me. The way it turned out though, I'm not sure. The teacher said, "He's a little feverish. Just a minute." Then she put a cold cloth on my forehead and down over my eyes, but she didn't get my left eye completely covered. If the other eye hadn't been fully covered that would have been some sight.

Well, anyway, I didn't mean to tell you so much about the doctor's boy. You'll learn that preachers' kids have to keep their mouths shut. Anyway, we walked on up past the fence made with iron pipes stuck through concrete posts. Then we went across the corner to the preacher's house.

His house was big and brick where ours was little and wooden. There were a lot of rooms. Some of his family had a whole room to themselves. Sister Sisk said, "Well, look who's here." She acted like it was all a big surprise. She may have fooled the girls, but I knew it wasn't something that came up all of a sudden.

Everybody behaved pretty good. I pushed the kids in the swing a lot. It was an old tire on the end of a rope tied to a tree limb. The tree was on the side of a hill so when you swung to the downhill side you were pretty high up. I finally got a turn on the swing. The little ones couldn't push me much so I swung myself real high. Then I jumped out at the highest point of the swing. The preacher's wife gave me what for 'cause her two boys were happy to learn that trick. She said a bigger preacher's boy shouldn't teach other kids to do things like that.

You'll learn, little PK, that there're a lot of things you aren't supposed to do. There're a few that you have to do too. One of them is to eat the fat in your minced ham. It was bad to have to sit at the Sisk's table and watch Betty pick the white spots out of her meat. Mrs. Sisk said, "My land, Child. Do you always do that?"

She doesn't always do that 'cause we sure don't have much minced ham. We have fat pork belly, lots of it. Maybe that is why Betty didn't want the little bits of fat. Anyway, it was strange sleeping in an upstairs bedroom and looking out and down the street this morning to see the doctor's car at our house.

I'm glad you got born so we could come home.

8

Memo 2: The Relief Order

You're growing. Mom and Dad won't let me get my hands on you very much. I have to sit in the rocker and then Mom lays you in my arms for a little bit. You're kinda hard to hold onto.

I get to do some things for you, though. Like run the water in the tub the night before your diapers are washed. We have to let the water heat a little—the tub is set on bricks and we build a fire under it. When its heated we put sal soda in it. Helps break the hard water, they say. Anyway, the next morning there is a scum on the water that we skim off. That way, when Mom scrubs your diapers on the board they come out white.

I have to run the water from the faucet into a bucket. Then it is carried over to the tub and poured in. Some folks have a hose, but we haven't been able to buy one yet.

Another thing I do for you is haul in your groceries. You didn't do so good nursing for some reason. Maybe no more than she eats, Mom just didn't have enough milk for you. Anyway, there is more to haul home with each grocery order these days.

On Thursdays I go to a lady's house and get the relief order. I made a mistake the other day and didn't notice the new sign on her front door. It said, *Relief orders are available at the backdoor only*. I didn't see the sign and rang the front doorbell. Her oldest boy opened the door and said, "Can't you read? Now get off of our front porch and go around to the back or you won't get any order."

I felt like saying, "Who wants a relief order? I came to invite you to church." But I knew I had to get that order, so when he slammed the door I went around the house. The backdoor was open when I got there and the lady was writing out the form. She didn't say anything. I didn't have to wait long like I sometimes did. She seemed very nervous. Her hand was shaking when she gave me the papers. She patted my shoulder as I left, but she wouldn't look at me while she was in the choir the next Sunday.

On Friday Mom goes over the handbills from the store so she can make out the grocery list. Friday afternoon or Saturday morning I take it to the store. We get a lot of dried beans and a lot of canned beef. We always get a lot of canned milk and big boxes of dried milk. Now we get a lot more of this since you've come. You get the canned milk as long as it lasts, then you get powdered milk like the rest of us. You get Karo syrup in your milk. Some kids get Eagle Brand milk, but I guess none of us ever did.

The grocery order sure fills up my wagon. You can ride in my wagon when you get a little bigger. I'll be glad to pull you. You won't be near as heavy as those groceries. They are in boxes and bags and they are piled pretty high. When we get eggs they go on top and they keep slipping like they just want to fall off.

From the store I go up Main Street to the filling station. I can pull the wagon down their slanting drive to the street so it doesn't bump off of the curb. Across the street is the Methodist church. I don't hurry past there like I used to just to keep from getting sprinkled on.

The next half block is downhill, then the following block is uphill. I don't know which is worse, going downhill with the wagon bumping my heels or having to pull so hard going uphill. After that hill it's pretty easy. There are driveways that can be used so I don't have to worry anymore about curbs. If a wheel doesn't come off, I'm home free.

When you get old enough I'll show you how to keep the wheels on coaster wagons. The wheels slip on the ends of axles made of an iron rod with a hole sideways through the end of them. You put a thing called a cotter pin through the hole after you put the wheel on to keep it on. My problem is that the cotter pins wore out and I have to use wire. It is soft and wears out too easy.

The hubcaps are gone too. They cover up the ends of the axles. As long as I had one hubcap, I kept it on the right rear wheel 'cause when you are coasting by pushing with your right foot you can hit your ankle on the end of the axle. That takes off a piece of hide. If your ankle isn't healed from the last time you hurt it, you can knock the scab off real easy.

The last time I hurt my foot that way was up by the school superintendent's house. He didn't feel sorry 'cause I was crying. He just heard what I said when I first hurt it. He said, "I ought to tell your father on you for talking like that. He will wash out your mouth with soap."

You will learn that preacher's kids have to watch their language more than other kids do. You better help me wish that if I do get told on that Daddy doesn't put that sal soda in the water before he washes my mouth out.

Memo 3: Store Work

I haven't been able to spend as much time with you as I want to. You sleep a lot. Also, I am now working at the grocery store. The manager and I got pretty well acquainted filling those relief orders. Sometimes he would get busy and I would sack the potatoes and beans or grind the coffee or bring the sack of flour from the back room. It was fun to do this and he said, "That shows you have initiative. I like that." So you grow yourself some initiative while you are growing up. It seems to be a pretty good thing for preacher's kids to have.

After school on Wednesday another fellow and I get the handbills ready to mail out to the rural routes. We fold the bills a couple of times and put a staple in them. Then they have to be stamped with a big rubber stamp that says "Boxholder, Rural Route No._____." We fix hundreds of them then write in 1 or 2 or 3 in the blank space for the route number. Then we lick postage stamps and stick them on. The glue tastes awful. We can't waste any stamps for any reason, so if we tear one in two we have to stick the pieces on real careful, like working a jigsaw puzzle.

If we have time, we candle eggs. When a farmer brings in eggs to sell we have to count them first. Then we turn on a light in a box with a hole in it. We put the egg over the hole and if the egg is good it looks a pretty orange-pink color. If it is a bad egg, it is all black. We don't count the bad eggs when we figure how many to pay the farmer for. Sometimes they say, "I candled those eggs and there weren't any bad ones." Then the store manager says he wants to see the bad ones. We show him and he puts them in a sack to give back to the farmer. Some of those farmers go to churches where Daddy preaches. You will learn that going to church won't keep people from trying to sell bad eggs.

When the big truck comes in each week, we have to stack groceries in the back room. The alley where the truck stops is way up high and the back room is very low. We put a sliding board from the truck to the floor of the room. Then boxes of canned goods and sacks of flour are slid down the board. They come down real fast. When they stop sliding we pick them up and stack them. Sometimes my back hurts before we get the truck unloaded. The truck driver talks awful, especially when a sack of flour hits a nail and rips open. He ought to go to Sunday School more often.

On Thursdays I pass out the handbills in our half of town. This is fun unless it is very hot or raining. I don't have a raincoat so I get pretty wet. The bills get wet too. We go to the printing office and get a big stack of bills on Wednesday. After we fix a lot of them for the mail, there are a lot left for passing out. The bills smell like the printing office, which is a good smell. By the time the bills are all passed my hands are black from the ink and smell kind of like the printing office.

Some of the ladies are waiting for the bills. The ladies don't like for the bills to blow off the porch so we have to stick them in the door. Some of the men don't like for us to give out the advertising at their houses. One man said, "My old lady spends too d___ much for groceries already without you coming around here." He didn't go to our church or I would tell our preacher on him for cussing.

Sacking sugar, beans, and coffee is a lot of fun. They all come in big, hundred-pound sacks which the men haul up to the scales for us. We open the big sack then weigh the stuff as we put it in paper sacks. Sugar and beans go into five- and ten-pound brown sacks. The coffee goes into one- and three-pound sacks that are printed in colors. We have to weigh the coffee beans and then grind them into the sack. The grinder is electric, but we have a big, old, hand-cranked grinder to use if the regular one breaks down. The coffee sure smells good.

I don't get to help the butcher very much. He says kids don't keep their hands clean enough to touch meat. Sometimes he lets me slice baloney on the electric slicer. It is very sharp and I have to be very careful. I like to work for the butcher. He teases me a lot. Daddy is usually so serious and worried that he doesn't tease. He sometimes reads to us out of the joke book, though. Most of the time he reads the Bible.

The butcher spends a lot of time talking to the lady who runs the restaurant. She buys more meat than any other customer. This makes the butcher like her a lot, but I think he just plain likes her.

Preacher's kids have to be careful what they say whether they mean anything bad or not. Like the other day when the butcher was teasing me. He said I was a little kid and talked too much and didn't work hard enough for my money. I wasn't sure he was teasing and I didn't want the manager to hear him talking like that. So I said to him, "If you don't quit talking to me like that, I'll tell the lady from the restaurant that you pick on little kids."

"That won't do you any good," he said. "She doesn't cut any ice around here."

"Oh no?" one of the big clerks said.

"You stay out of this," the butcher told him. "I'm talking to Little Preach here."

"If you don't let me alone," I told him, "I won't tell you what the restaurant lady said about you."

He got real interested right away. The manager and the other fellows up front got real interested too. They stopped working and looked back at me and the butcher.

"What did she say?" Butch asked.

"I ain't gonna tell you."

"If you don't, I'll stick your head in the pickle barrel."

"You'd better not."

"She didn't say anything, I betcha," Butch said.

"Yes, she did." I was trying to figure out what to tell him 'cause she really hadn't said anything.

"What was it?"

Well, I was really on a spot. I was talking too big for my britches. Mom had been warning me about doing that. Well, the butcher wasn't acting very big, picking on a little kid. So I told him, "She said you ain't big enough in the britches."

I thought the butcher would croak. He got red and then he got purple. The clerks might near died laughing and the manager was getting a chuckle out of it too. He said, "Well, Butch, anything else you want to know?"

Butch just said, "Darn bigmouthed kid." He didn't stick my head in the pickle barrel.

I really don't know what was so funny about that. You'll just have to learn that grown-ups take some things different than you mean them. They seem to know things kids don't so I guess you must have to wait until you grow up to know what it is all about.

It isn't all bad, though. One of the clerks gave me a baloney and cracker sandwich and a bottle of orange soda.

Butch doesn't talk to the restaurant lady as much as he used to.

P.S.—I get $1.42 a week for all of my work. I think I'll save it and buy something big. My tithe is 14¢. It figures out pretty good with no tithe on 2¢.

Memo 4: Swiss Chard

Mom had me pick the Swiss chard out of the garden and sell it to the store. There was a bushel of it. We got a dollar and a half for it 'cause it was a heaping full basket. So you may get some new clothes soon. Most of your things are hand-me-downs. Some of them Mom had, but a lot of them were given to us by neighbors or people from the church.

I got in trouble over trying to sell the Swiss chard for spinach. Mom just got to calling it spinach so we called it spinach when it was on the table. She put egg slices on it. We poured some vinegar on it like it was spinach. So when I asked the store manager if he would buy a bushel of spinach he said OK.

Mom washed the leaves after I picked them. Then we packed them in the basket, being careful not to break them or crush them too tight. Then I hauled the whole thing up to the store.

The manager came out to the wagon in front of the store. He took one look and said, "Where is the spinach?"

I told him it was right there.

He said, "I don't see any spinach. That green stuff you got there is Swiss chard. Everybody has it in their own garden. You shouldn't a wasted your time haulin' it up here."

"Well, I thought it was spinach. Can't you sell it, anyhow?" I asked.

Then he said the government food inspector would get me some day for mislabeling food. He said all I had to do was read the name on the seed package when I planted the stuff. But I didn't plant it. Dad was afraid I'd get too many of those little seeds in one place so I planted potatoes and he planted the spinach, Swiss chard.

Anyway, the manager said he'd take the stuff, whatever it was, and put it in the produce window. If it sold, he would pay for it. If it didn't, he'd throw it out into the back alley. So he put the Swiss chard in the window. I sprinkled some water on it, and it looked real green and fresh.

The next day it wasn't in the window so I checked the alley; it wasn't out there either. Then I went in the store where the manager said we were pretty lucky and gave me the dollar and a half.

So, you will probably get some new diapers or something. And when you get big enough for overalls and selling stuff out of the garden, you better learn what all of it is. Some preachers just don't know spinach from Swiss chard and I'm afraid your daddy is one of them.

By now you should know who I am and something of what I do, and I sure hope you like me.

II.   Grade Schools

The institutions, other than the church, that had the most influence on my life were the grade schools. And as most preacher's kids do, I attended a lot of them. They were in small Southern Illinois towns. The first grade was attended in Cobden, the second in Vienna, third and fourth in Tamms, fifth, sixth, and seventh in Anna, and then back to Cobden for the eighth grade.

Dedicated schoolteachers did much to mold my life. Many of them were members of the churches that Dad pastored. Some of them were Sunday School teachers.

Today I can think of no greater opportunity to improve the American way of life than to be both a grade school and Sunday School teacher. Before I was able to have strong thoughts of my own, Mother, Dad, and teachers molded my thinking. They directed me into paths of learning, exploring, loving, living, and growing. They opened to me a whole world that was centered around our home and church but that was created by a great and loving God.

Some of the lessons I learned during this grade school period came from breaking the rules. This can be an uncomfortable but unforgettable way of learning.

I tried to spare my little brother some of the hard knocks.

Memo 5: A Demonstration Bout

There are some rules that are sure hard to understand. After you learn what the rules are, you have to learn to follow them even though you don't understand why they are the way they are. Even though you don't believe the rule is correct, you have to obey it.

Like today when I had a fight and didn't know an important rule. It was embarrassing and I had a tough time winning, and it wouldn't have taken long to whip the guy without that silly rule.

In physical education we started taking boxing lessons. The coach asked if anyone had ever boxed before. My friend Art said he had. He wanted me as his sparring partner, so the coach asked me, "Have you ever had any fights?"

Now, he didn't know much about preacher's kids or he wouldn't have asked a question like that. I thought about the O'Toole kids down where we used to live and said, "Yep."

The next thing I knew Art and I were in the ring and the boxing gloves were being laced on. The coach said we had to stand in opposite corners and come out boxing when he blew the whistle. We would fight for one minute then he would blow the whistle for us to stop. We would rest a minute then start the next round. I don't remember how many rounds we were supposed to box because we didn't need all of them before we finished the demonstration.

It was sort of funny standing there in the corner waiting for the first whistle. It seemed like such a waste of time. We had the gloves on. Instead of staying close together so we could get started we were standing farther apart. Instead of blowing the whistle, the coach was standing there looking at Art, who had his hands up and out front of him, and me leaning back against the rope with my hands, gloves, on my hips.

While we were just wasting time I got to thinking again about those O'Toole kids. There were four of them and they used to make it hot for me. Every time I went to town they would see me on the way to the store. They wouldn't do a thing then. Those sons of a gun would hide out until I started home with the things Mom had sent me for. I always had a sack or two of groceries or one sackful in one hand and a gallon can of coal oil in the other.

You can't do much with both hands busy like that. With one hand free you can pick up a rock or a board or a stick to even up the situation a little. If you have coal oil, it's especially bad. We lost the cap off the spout a long time ago so we just use a potato. If you run you can bump that potato off with your knee and then you get coal oil on your pants leg. You have to be careful to keep the smelly stuff from splashing on the groceries too. Of course, if you need to, you can throw that stinking potato. Or, if they get close, you can sock it into some guy's face. But usually you just have to run for home as fast as you can, with the rocks being thrown all around you.

The last time I had to do that the O'Tooles kept throwing rocks until I was inside the backdoor. Boy, when that gravel hit the washtubs hanging on the side of the house it really made a racket.

Those O'Tooles made me very mad, and I sure was kept busy catching them one at a time and keeping the score even. That oldest one egged the other ones on so I got the maddest at him. Just when I got to remembering him the coach blew the whistle.

Art came dancing over, stabbing his left arm back and forth and taking a kind of jig step. That looked pretty sissified to me, and I was already worked up thinking about the O'Tooles so I belted Art up side the head. It caught him by surprise, I think. He must have been looking for me to crouch or wiggle back and forth, but I just flung one straight from my hip to his head.

He flopped over on the floor so I sat down straddle of his tummy and punched a few quick ones to his nose and face. The coach yelled bloody murder and kept blowing his whistle. It sure seemed like a short round, but I quit anyway.

The coach was really mad. He hollered and asked if I knew the rules? "You don't strike your opponent when he is down. You go to a neutral corner and stay there until he gets up or until the count of ten."

Little as you are, you can understand how silly that is. Just when you are about to win you have to turn the guy loose. But that is the rule. I suppose it's so the fights will last longer so when people pay to see real prize fights they will get their money's worth.

Coach sent us to our corners again. Then he blew his whistle. I was sort of confused. I didn't know whether we were restarting the first round or beginning the second. As it turned out it didn't make any difference.

We'd wasted so much time because I hadn't known the rule I thought I had better hurry so we could catch up. I sort of half ran and half jogged toward Art's corner. At about midring my right hand came off my hip and I aimed it at Art's head again. He must have changed his mind about demonstrating boxing then 'cause he climbed through the ropes and fell off the edge of the ring. Coach blew his whistle, lifted one of my hands up, and swatted me on the hind end with his other hand.

He said, "Looks like you're the winner, Tiger. We have to teach you a thing or two, but I think we can make a boxer out of you." Now I'm shadow boxing and punching a bag, but its not very much fun.

I thought Art would be pretty mad at me for being so dumb about the rules and all. He's been real friendly, though. He has some fellows who used to rough him up like the O'Toole kids did me. He says since they know he's a boxer who knows the rules they are letting him alone. He has me walk to school and back with him so he can show me how nice they are being.

He's right, 'cause they haven't picked on him at all while I've been with him to watch what's going on. I don't think it's 'cause Art's a boxer, though. I think it's 'cause I know their preacher, and they are afraid I'll tell on them.

Memo 6: Flagpole Ornament

If you ever get moved from the *A* class in school to the *B* class, don't try to hide it from Mom and Dad. You can't, so don't ever try to fib about it either. Oh, you won't want to hurry home and yell out loud, "Guess what, I got moved down from 6*A* to 6*B.*" What you can do is wait until everybody is feeling pretty good about the end of supper. Then kind of offhand say, "I was expecting them to move me back to 6*B,* and they did it today."

Like I said, don't try to hide it. As sure as you do, some kid will tell his folks who know somebody in the family and they will ask Mom and Dad, "What's the matter with Junior that he got put down?"

It all started because the heels were wearing out on my high top boots and we don't have any magazines. Let me explain that to you.

My high tops—the shoes with the knife pocket on the side of the right one—have big, tough heels. It takes a good-sized nail to hold those heels on. So when the heels get worn way down, an awful lot of nail scratches the floor under my desk at school. The janitor knows that most of those two furrows under there were dug by my heels 'cause there is fresh, clean wood showing.

Well, the janitor showed the damage to old Mrs. Clutts, my homeroom and geography teacher. She came back to tell me I should get my heels fixed. That's when she saw I didn't have much done on my geography notebook about Africa. That notebook is causing a big problem. It is supposed to have pictures of houses, animals, people, mountains, rivers, and a whole lot more. Most of the kids in the class have magazines at home, or their neighbors do. We haven't got money for magazines and neither do most of the people who live by us. There are pictures in the books and magazines in the library, but you can't cut them out.

I tried to explain this to Mrs. Clutts but she didn't care. She makes more than Dad does and besides that she gets paid on payday. Her husband works too. So I guess if she wants magazines she gets them.

Anyway, I didn't finish that notebook and got a *D* in geography that put me over into 6*B*. The kids in there are pretty nice and a lot of them don't mind being there. But I want out and not just because the copper flush float from a toilet tank got put on top of the flagpole in place of the shiny brass ball. The top of the flagpole is just outside the 6*B* windows. The longer it stays there the madder the principal gets. But I want back in 6*A* because my other grades are good, and I belong there.

That flush float makes it hard for me to study sometimes. I look up and look out there and have to grin. So many people keep guessing wrong about who put it up there and how it was put there.

Some folks think somebody climbed up the pole. When someone else points out that the pole would bend from a person's weight, someone else says, "They could have tied on guide ropes as they went up." And the coach said, "Some little wiry guy like Smitty could climb it and not bend it over very far."

It made me feel funny when he said that. It was like he was accusing me of climbing the pole, but I didn't. Nobody else climbed it either.

Another idea was that the flagpole was jacked up out of the concrete base and then stood up again. That's a silly idea. That would be a lot of work and the guys who put that float up there aren't too work brittle.

One day during recess Mr. Johnson walked over to where we were playing pitching washers and talking about a lot of things. Somehow we got to talking about the flagpole, Mr. Johnson just talking like everybody else.

Somewhere in all of that talking he looked at me and said, "David, if you were going to put that float up there, how would you do it?"

That was a pretty roundabout way of sneaking up on my blind side, but even if I didn't see him coming, I knew when he got there. "I didn't put that float up there," I told him.

"Oh, I understand that," he said. "But if you had to do it, how would you go about it?"

"Well, if I had it to do—which you understand I didn't—I would climb up the fire escape, that's on that side of the building and lasso the top of the pole with a rope. I'm not strong enough—I don't think I'm strong enough—to pull it over to the fire escape, but a couple of high school guys probably could manage it without too much trouble."

"Especially if they had somebody to change the ornament while they held the pole still?" he asked.

He was getting pretty tricky with his questions.

"They wouldn't need nobody else if they tied that old pole to the fire escape with a short rope," I suggested.

"You're right, they probably wouldn't," he said.

He kept looking at me like he expected me to keep talking.

"They'd have a problem, though, if they weren't careful how they let loose of the rope."

"What do you mean?"

"Well, that old pole would fly back away from there mighty fast, and might fling the float right off of its top."

"How far would it go?" he wanted to know. "All the way to the road?"

"Probably farther than that, Mr. Johnson. I'll bet it would go all the way over into the ball field on the other side."

"You seem to be pretty sure of that," he said, and by then he was grinning real big.

I sort of smiled too. "Pretty sure. And then they'd have to do the job all over again and let the pole back out easy with the long rope with a slip knot in it so they could get the rope back off of the pole."

The bell rang then so we had to quit talking and go back to class. That night the principal went to Judy and Fuzzy's house, and someone gave him the brass ball for the flagpole. The janitor put it back on by using two ropes just like I told Mr. Johnson the job could be done. He even used a short rope for tying the pole to the fire escape while the other man welded the ball to the pole.

On Friday I was told to move back to 6*A* the next Monday. I even got my same desk back. Guess they didn't want me digging new holes in the floor with my boot heels which aren't fixed yet. They already have holes in the floor in both 6*A* and 6*B*. The worst thing about those heels is that they can easily trip a fellow if he's in a hurry to get down a fire escape to fetch a copper flush float back up from the ball field.

Memo 7: The Circular Fire Escape

It isn't a very good arrangement when you live by the school you attend, have your school desk near the fire escape door, and have some of the girls in your class go to the same Sunday School you do. When the girls' mothers know your Mom that makes it even worse.

First, my desk is uncomfortably close to the fire escape. If I hurry I can be the first one out the little emergency door. When I don't hurry now, some other people don't want to go first. That's because when I didn't hurry and get there first during a fire drill, the girls who went first got shook up a little bit. Some people think I know when to hurry or not to hurry, and sometimes they may be right.

You see, our fire escape in 6*A* is not an open set of stairs made of iron grillwork. It is like a sheet metal silo with a tube that goes round and round and down inside of it. It's sort of an enclosed corkscrew slicky slide. There is a door at the bottom that flies open when the first person down the slide hits the inside of the door with his feet.

Up on our floor the emergency door opens onto a short platform with guardrails. The door into the fire escape will open to the inside if you push on a knob on the outside.

When the fire bell rings we go through the emergency door, across the platform, push in the fire escape entrance door, slide around and down, bang the bottom door, and pop right out. That is, the first one out opens the door. The rest of the class just follows behind and has fun sliding down.

It's so much fun sliding down the fire escape that we play in it some weekends. Someone climbs up the corner of the building to the second floor and then walks across the ledge to the platform. Then he slides down and opens the bottom door. After that we climb up the inside of the fire escape and slide back down.

When the escape hasn't been used for a while it gets a little rusty and dirty. We usually think to slide down on a rag first to clean it. Sometimes Mom can tell by the seat of my pants that we forgot the rag and I had to go first.

Sometimes some kids do some dirty things in the fire escape, but we don't do that. We know the kids who live close to the school will get blamed for everything. Our problem was bread wrappers.

To help us get a fast slide we try different things like sliding on a board or a cloth. But nothing adds speed like a piece of waxed paper or a bread wrapper. By the time we use bread wrappers for slides all day Saturday and Sunday afternoon, the fire escape gets pretty slick.

That's what had happened the weekend before we had a fire drill on Monday. So when the bell rang I knew we would all get a fast ride and I really wanted to go first. But those boot heels I told you about earlier got caught on the desk legs and almost made me fall out into the aisle. Several kids got in line ahead of me.

Little old Mary Alice got shoved out the door first. To hear her tell it she sure flew down the slippery spiral. The janitor said she came out straightened out flat with her dress tail up and flopped right out on the ground. That knocked the breath out of her and the next kid almost landed on her. I shoved my boots against the sides of the slide for brakes and came out standing up.

By then old Mary Alice had her breath back and started screaming. When I came out she saw me and yelled, "Its all your fault, Junior Smith. You greased that slide or you would have been first."

A whole bunch of the other kids, especially the girls, began yelling the same thing. The janitor heard them and some of the teachers did too.

I had to explain to the teacher that we sometimes played in the fire escape and that a whole bunch had been in it that weekend. She just said, "Don't do it anymore."

At church old Mary Alice was still limping around and taking on so people would pay attention to her. Then her mother said to Mom, "Sister Smith, I guess you know your boy hurt my Mary Alice in the fire escape?"

First I had a hard time explaining that I wasn't playing in the fire escape with Mary Alice. Then I had to tell about how the bread wrappers work. I tried to tell Mom it was either use the wrappers or get my pants rusty, but she said I had no business in that fire escape in the first place.

She may be right, but that doesn't keep it from being fun.

Memo 8: Masculine Bear

Some girls just don't like some boys. There are some situations that seem to make them dislike you even more. If the girl's mother or father is a schoolteacher and you are a preacher's son, that makes things worse. If the girl is just ahead of you on the honor roll, she'll think you are going to catch up with her next month, and she won't like that. And if you help her with her art project when she doesn't want help, things will get a lot worse in a hurry. '

Dottie makes better grades than I do some months. Her seat is across the aisle and one seat back from mine. I think she would like me better if I didn't sit so close. However, I think it is a pretty good arrangement because there are times when I want to say something to her. Especially when she is acting uppity.

She beat me on the honor roll last month so she has been acting very smart. I think I was just trying to help her with her water coloring, but maybe I was just trying to get even with her. Anyway, I added a little sex to her picture.

I don't know much about sex yet except that you don't talk about it except to boys your own age or older and only when no grown ups are listening. When you can't even talk about something, you sure better not include it in your art.

What happened was that we were drawing pictures of animals and water-coloring them. Dottie was making a picture of a bear, probably a grizzly, and I was painting a kangaroo.

Some of the class were teasing me because my kangaroo was a momma. She didn't have any babies—not in the picture, anyway— but she had a pouch. Now a pouch isn't sexy. A kangaroo is a m-a-r-s-u-p-i-a-l and carries her babies in a pouch. An opossum is a— the same thing. She has a pouch, but spends a lot of time carrying her babies on her back with their tails wrapped around her big tail. A kangaroo's pouch is no more sexy than an opossums' tail that's right out in the open for every one to see, so it can't be very sexy.

Dottie's bear was something else. She went to the washroom and left that bear on top of her desk. I was surprised at the neutral look it had. It was standing straight up on its hind legs with its front paws out like it was begging. Just by looking you couldn't tell if it were a girl bear or a boy bear.

I just happened to be painting my kangaroo brown, so with one short brush stroke Dottie's bear became a he bear. Then Dottie came back to her seat.

She took one look and let out a mighty shriek. "David Smith, you ruined my bear," she yelled. "You have utterly ruined it. I'm so embarrassed."

"What makes you think I did it?" I wanted to know.

"You are painting with brown paint."

"Well, look around, why don't you? A lot of people in this room are a painting with brown paint." Thank goodness, they were.

"You did it. You did it."

Mr. Johnson heard the racket and came back to see what all the fuss was about. When Dottie showed him the bear, he grinned a little first, then he looked serious.

"It does look like a masculine bear."

That word is a tough one, but you can look up *masculine* in the dictionary sometime. Or Dad has a book called *R-o-g-e-t-'s T-h-e-s-a-u-r-u-s.* It isn't much for definitions but has a lot of other words that mean the same. Dad uses it when he writes sermons so he can choose the big words that mean the same as the little ones that don't sound so important.

Anyway, Mr. Johnson suggested that Dottie could paint over part of the bear's tummy so it wouldn't look so much like a he bear. She said she would try because it would sure take a lot of time to draw and paint another whole bear.

All during the next art period Dottie worked on that bear. She made so much of a to-do about it that nearly all the girls got to watching her. Before long they were all giggling except Dottie. She kept looking more exasperated all the time. Finally they made so much noise that Mr. Johnson came back for another look.

"Well, Dottie, now your bear looks very, very feminine. In fact she looks very, very pregnant," he said.

There are two more words for you to look up. They will lead to some other interesting words.

I thought it was funny, but I didn't even laugh out loud. I just looked the other way and grinned a little. That Dottie. She got mad at me for using just a little bit of paint and a little teeny minute's worth of time to make her bear look a little masculine. She took a lot of time and a lot of paint to make her bear look really feminine.

That just goes to show you you can't figure out the thinking of girls who are uppity and who get mad at you.

Memo 9: Hot Frame, Cold Frame

There are a lot of glass covered beds of growing things out in the country from our town. There are some small ones in town where ladies start flowers early in the spring. I have never been able to tell for sure which one is which—hot frame or cold frame.

This caused me to be very embarrassed in science class one day. Mr. Johnson asked someone to describe a—I think it was a hot frame—but he said he couldn't. Next he called on me. I was sure I had it all figured out, so I described one in great detail.

They start building a hot frame by digging two or three ditches about twenty or thirty or even fifty feet long. Tiles are laid in the ditches. At one end the tile is run into a pit where a wood fire can be built. At the other end the tiles go together at the bottom of a vertical tile for a chimney. A bed of very good soil is spread over the ditches. A frame at least a foot high is built all around the soil bed and a glass frame cover goes over the whole thing.

When a fire is built in the pit, heat and smoke go through the tile and out the chimney. This warms the soil to give plants a good start while the weather is still cold. Some days are warm and no fire is needed, but on cold nights a small fire may be started to keep away the frost.

I thought I did a good job describing the frame, but Mr. Johnson said I was all wrong. He made a big thing of asking everybody in class the same question. He said we were sure a bunch of town kids 'cause none of us knew the answer.

To make sure we would know the next time the question was asked, he arranged for us to go to a farm and look at a hot frame. We had a good time making the trip. The frame looked just like I said it would except it didn't have a fire pit or a chimney.

We all stood around while Mr. Johnson and the farmer took off the glass cover. Inside the frame was very dark, rich-looking soil. Sweet potato plants were going to be started in the frame.

At Mr. Johnson's instruction we all knelt down around the sides of the frame. He said, "Feel the soil. Isn't it warm?"

I had one hand sticking in the dirt a little ways and it was warm. "What makes the soil warm?" Mr. Johnson asked.

Most of us guessed that it was the sun shining through the glass frame.

"That's not correct," Mr. Johnson said. "Take a good feel of the bed material. Get both hands in there and rub the soil between them."

By then I was enjoying the warmth and had leaned over up to my elbows in dirt.

"That's horse manure," Mr. Johnson said.

Boy, I sure came up from there like a shot. Every other guy in the gang did too. There we stood looking at our hands and arms and each other. Luckily, the stuff didn't stick to our skin. We sniffed and it really didn't smell bad. There were some mighty peculiar expressions around that frame, whatever kind it was.

Mr. Johnson was doubled over with laughter and the farmer was having a fit like he was in on the joke from the start.

"Now, can anyone in the class tell me how to build a hot frame?"

We all finally had a good laugh and went to the pump to wash our hands. Then we all had an apple the farmer had left over from last fall. Most of us were careful to hold the apple by the ends of the core while we ate it.

The next time we got together in class the teacher explained that horse manure and soil were warmed by heat formed by the decaying manure. This made the soil rich and warm. With a little added moisture and protected by the glass cover, it made an ideal early season growing bed.

Most of the new sweet potato plants were started in this kind of bed. Thousands of them are grown around our country and are shipped all over the country. Some farmers make a lot of money growing slips, as the new sweet potato plants are called.

Later in the spring I made some spending money picking slips for transplanting. A big sweet potato is planted in the warm soil bed and is kept moist. Sprouts come out all over it and shoot up through the loose soil. To pick them you slip your fingers down into the dirt and pinch the shoot off up next to the potato.

It's hard to imagine that a great big potato vine that will grow lots of sweet potatoes started out as a small slip from a potato buried in horse manure. Maybe it's like Dad said when I told him about picking plants and wondering if they would grow. He said, "Don't worry about that. A lot of big men used to be mere slips of boys who started out in worse environments than that."

Memo 10: Three-day Measles

Around churches you hear a lot about, "It's more blessed to give than to receive." Generally that is true, but in case of the measles it's not so. Especially for preacher's kids. If any kid in our family goes to church with the measles or anything else that's catching, Mom and Dad are sure to hear about it.

Since this is so, Mom is always checking us. If we rub an eye too much and it gets red, she has to make sure we don't have pink eye. Scratch a mosquito bite until it bleeds on Monday and it better be healed and the scab off by next Sunday. If it isn't, some lady will swear the preacher's kids have "emphatygoe" (impetigo). I think they call it that. Or maybe it's infant eye—oh, I don't know.

Any kind of food rash gets blown up to be smallpox, chicken pox, or most any other kind of pox. It seems that different pox have rashes that start at different places on your body. Some start on the back, some on the neck, and most on the tummy. A preacher's son in the Nursery, Beginner, or Primary Departments has no privacy at all. By the time you get to be a Junior all the teachers in those departments have seen your tummy a dozen times.

You can expect to have your shirttail pulled out of your pants and your tummy looked at in public till you get into junior high or can dodge and run pretty fast.

And you know where we get all those nice things? That's right. We get them at church from the kids of all those women who are always checking our tummies.

I thought by now I was old enough not to hear anything about my giving the German measles to somebody, but it didn't work out that way. I broke out with them on Saturday, so I didn't go to church on Sunday at all. They didn't make me sick. The three days were up on Tuesday, but Mom made me wait until Thursday to go to school.

Nothing happened Thursday and I went to basketball practice

that afternoon. Coach made me take it easy. About halfway through practice I got a little tired, but I didn't feel too bad.

Friday night we had two games. I'm not on the first five on the regular squad so I get to play all the second-team game and about half the first team game. We won the second-team game pretty easy so I really didn't get too warmed up.

That first team game was something else. Those Carbondale guys are big. They know how to play ball too. We managed to keep up with them, and by playing hard, we got a little ahead. I keep saying "we" because one of the guards turned his ankle in the second quarter and I got into the game.

At halftime I was rather tuckered out. Coach saw me looking a little puny and said, "What's the matter, Smitty, the measles getting to you?"

"Naw, just two games in a row got me winded for a minute," I told him. But you know, I began to get a little worried. I thought I could see some of those measle spots beginning to show up again.

About the end of the third quarter I was really feeling tough. I was hot and sweaty, and by then it seemed a sure thing those old measle bumps were popping back out. One of the big old Carbondale forwards tried to run over me to attempt a shot so I slammed into him pretty hard. Gene, the referee, called a foul on me.

Somehow I ended up with the ball, so it was up to me to toss it to Gene. I didn't think he should have called a foul on me, and then he turned away from me just as I started to toss him the ball. Without thinking, I guess I threw the ball harder than necessary. It hit Gene in the back of the head. Boy, did he turn around and glare at me.

"What you want me to do, carry it around all night or toss it back to you?"

"I don't want you to hit me with it," he growled.

"Should have stayed looking and caught it," I told him.

He wasn't sure whether it was an accident or on purpose so he let it go. Coach knew it wasn't an accident, though, 'cause he'd seen me getting mad. He was laughing hard by then since he knew I was getting by without a technical or being thrown out of the game.

Coach left me in for a few more plays and then took me out of the game. He motioned for me to sit by him. He put a towel over my shoulders and said real quiet like, "We'd better cover up those measles and let you cool off. I thought you said you were over them."

"I thought I was but they popped back out."

"Well, they're pretty plain now and will look worse when you take your shower. Why don't you shower now so the guys don't see you? Then go sit in my car. I'll take you home."

Now that was one time having measles in public worked out all right. We won the games. I got a ride home instead of walking and got out of church two Sundays on one case of three-day measles.

Memo 11: It Takes Two to Fight

There are times when you can get in trouble by just having a friend. I got in trouble because Arnie is my friend or maybe it was because Van isn't Arnie's friend. Anyway, they had a fight and I almost got a licking from the school principal because of it.

Arnie and Van had been itching for a fight for a long time. They always walked in the same crowd coming home from school. Just leaving school, while the teachers can still see us, nobody does very much. Oh, there is a little bit of shoving and elbowing going on but no real rough stuff.

A few blocks from the edge of the school grounds, we cross the highway. It seems like being careful crossing there keeps everyone serious. Then things break loose. Pretty soon someone gets tripped. If there is an apple core left in a lunch box, it gets thrown. Yesterday someone had an apple core, and Arnie got it up alongside the head. He thought Van did it, so he shoved him down the steps by the dry goods store.

Then Arnie and Van started jawing at each other real hard. None of us had a nickle for a cone when we walked by the newsstand. That might have cooled us off. Whoever gets cones lets the rest of the gang take licks.

At the post office Arnie and Van and me didn't get any mail for our folks. If we had that might have kept our hands full. At least one of those two could have said, "I can't fight you now. I've got my hands full of mail."

When we crossed the tracks Van tripped Arnie, and the fight almost started right then. That's no place for a fight though 'cause the Floridian is running late sometimes, and you don't want to get in its way. Van said he didn't trip Arnie. "You just can't pick up your feet," he said.

I could see Arnie was pretty mad. He doesn't get mad for nothing, not that Arnie. He is little and he has red hair and the temper to go with it. He didn't do anything until we crossed the hard road and got close to the mill. Then he shoved Van over a log.

They got to shoving back and forth so that by the time we got to the middle of the vacant lot, their fists were all doubled up. Then all of a sudden they were really going at it.

They fell down and started rolling over, first one on top then the other. Then they got up and kept right on slugging.

Down they went again and this time Van's head hit a piece of flint and he got a big gash in the back of his noggin.

That stopped the fight. Van was bleeding and turning white around the mouth. Then he started running for home. "I'm going to tell my ma on you two guys."

Several of us looked at each other trying to figure out who went along with Arnie to equal "two guys." Somehow I had a funny feeling I knew I was going to be the other guy.

Sure enough, after supper Van's mother came to our house. She told Mom and Dad what a horrible fight it was. She really laid it on about us doubling up on her poor Van. She described the big gash in his head and the large chunk of flint I hit him with. The way she told it, Arnie and I knocked Van down. Arnie held him and I hit him with the rock. It sure was all a lie, and it took me a long time to convince Dad. Then I got the long lecture about being known by the company you keep.

Next day at school there was the devil to pay. Van's mother had told Mr. Newman, the principal, the same story she told Mom and Dad. He called all three of us into his office. And would you believe it, right there in front of all of us, Van swore I hit him with that rock.

At first I thought Arnie would speak up and say he trounced him by himself and didn't need any help. Arnie wasn't saying anything, though. He was sitting there with his teeth clenched just saying

"Yes, Sir" and "No, Sir" and trying to say them at the right time to get out of trouble.

After a while Mr. Newman sent us back to class. Nobody got a licking, but I knew that was too good to last. Soon the office lady came for me.

When I got set down in front of him, Mr. Newman said, "David, who started that fight?"

I would liked to have blamed Van for lying or Arnie for not getting me out of it. Suddenly I realized that old man was setting a trap for me. If I blamed one of them, especially Van, I was into it.

"Well, Mr. Newman, it takes two to make a fight. If either of those two hadn't been itchin' to get into one, there wouldn't have been no ruckus." And that was the truth.

He gave me a long look then sent me back to my seat. Immediately Van and Arnie were called and the paddling started. Neither of them was my friend for a few days after that.

III. Community Life

Whether we are aware of it or not, most of us live in more than one community. A minister's family is often acutely aware of the various communities in which their fellow church members live.

A very small town is often the first easily discernible community of which persons become aware. A few hundred people, a store, a post office, a gasoline station, a doctor, and a church make up a familiar basic community.

Similar communities coexist in larger towns and cities.

A group of churches make up a community. Sometimes we call them associations. In the Great Commission Jesus mentioned Jerusalem, Judea, and all the nations—communities.

Growing up in most communities is usually interesting and enjoyable. Learning to identify the various communities in which one lives can be a measure of personal growth.

I found many facets of community life to be fascinating, infuriating, educational, and almost always interesting. Rural and small town America have given birth to and educated many of the nation's great people.

Having grown up in a series of small communities, I don't claim greatness, but I do claim to have an abundance of insights. Some of them were related to my little brother in the following memos.

I'll bet you have known many similar situations and people.

Memo 12: Election Year

It will be a long time before you are interested in politics, and maybe you shouldn't worry about them until you have your own family. I did some work for the Democrats. They paid good money, but it may not have been too good for Dad.

Somebody left word at the store for the boys who passed out the handbills to go over to the newspaper office. When we got there we were given a whole stack of papers. They were printed to look like small newspapers, but all they had in them were pictures and good words about men running for election. They were all Democrats.

We were told to pass the papers out at the same places we usually handed the store bills. When we finished we were to go to the empty store building with a sign on it that said *Democratic Headquarters.*

That stack of papers was pretty heavy at the start. I thought a long time about putting some of them in a drain tile, but they would have caused trouble the next time it rained.

Some people wouldn't take the paper. They said, "Don't leave that dirty rag on my front porch." Some others said things like, "If those guys get in, my Uncle Harry will lose his job at the state hospital."

Anyway, I kept walking and handing them out and the stack got smaller and lighter all the time. Finally they were all gone and I went to the headquarters. There were a lot of people in there talking and smoking cigars and calling people on the phone. I stood around for a long time before anybody spoke to me. One man who had been watching me sort of growled around his cigar, "What can I do for you, kid?"

I told him I passed out the papers I was given at the newspaper office. He asked, "How many didja hand out?" He had me there 'cause I hadn't counted them. When I told him so he asked, "Well, where all did you pass them?"

At first I thought he meant who all took them, but I sure didn't want to tell him about all those people who wouldn't take a copy. "The whole southwest quarter of town," I told him. "From Main Street and the railraod tracks all the way to the edge of town." I wanted it to sound as big as possible.

He said, "That's a pretty big territory for a little kid."

"I do it every week. It wasn't nothing."

Then he reached into a drawer and got a roll of bills. I hadn't ever seen that much money before—at least not in the offering plate. Not even on foreign missions day or when we take up a special for the orphan's home. Then he peeled off three one dollar bills and gave every one of them to me.

I held those bills in front of me and looked at them for a long time. I had never had three dollars at one time. And I didn't have any quarters or a half dollar in case he wanted change. Boy, for just passing out papers I was going to get at least more than I got for one week passing bills, sacking beans and stuff, and candling eggs.

"What's the matter kid, ain't that enough?"

Wow, he wasn't going to ask for change! "Oh, it's plenty. It's enough." My mind was turning over, really turning. "Thanks. Thanks, a lot." I started to turn around and run out of there before he changed his mind, but then I had a thought.

"Mister, if you need some more papers you just call me, will you?"

"What will I call you?" His voice was still loud and gruff, but he was looking down at me and smiling.

"You can call me Junior, and you can tell them at the store again or tell them at my house. I'm Preacher Smith's kid."

"You a preacher's kid?"

"Yep." Now make something out of it, I thought.

"Your dad a Democrat?"

"I don't know," I said, and I really didn't.

"I'll bet he's a Republican and you just don't want to say."

"Nope, I don't know. He ain't a Democrat or a Republican or a Catholic or a Congregationalist. And he sure ain't no Holy Roller. He's a Baptist."

The man took his cigar out of his mouth and laughed out loud.

"You're all right, kid. You know some of them Baptists are Democrats too? I'll let you know when we need you again."

I ran all the way home and showed Dad the money and told him how I got it. He said, "Come here, Grace, and look at your rich son." Then he told me preachers had to be neutral in politics or it could start trouble in the church. He said not to pass out any more Democrat papers. When I said I ought to pass out Republican papers to even the score he said, "Well, maybe that would be the best way to do it."

So the way I figure it, the Republicans owe us three dollars to keep us neutral the way preacher's kids have to be. I'm keeping my eye on the rest of the vacant stores, looking out for *Republican Headquarters* sign. If I don't get the job, maybe you can earn three bucks in a couple more elections so Dad's family won't be favoring either party too much.

Memo 13: To the Fair

When Dad explains something to you real good, you had better listen. Sometimes his explaining sounds kind of like his preaching, and that is when you have to be extra careful. I have learned to tune out the sermons. Sometimes I do that when he is explaining things. That's when I get into trouble.

The whole trouble comes from having to go to church so much. We have moved around a lot, so Dad gets to preach the same sermons rather often. When I'm sitting there in church and he reads the Scripture, I listen to see which verse he picks for the text. That generally gives a clue to whether it's going to be a familiar sermon. If it is, then I sometimes get to thinking about other things.

Now that I'm almost a teenager and the weather is warm, I get to thinking about, _____. I'd better not tell you that yet. Anyway, I'd better get back to about Dad's explaining things.

Sometimes when he explains real hard stuff when he is preaching, like the sermons from Revelation (not Revelations), he makes considerable noise. Either he bangs his Bible or a songbook on the pulpit. It seems the harder it is to explain, the more he bangs. I've got to where I know when the bangs are coming.

When Dad starts working up to a bang I begin to quit thinking about other things. Right then is a good time to start looking at the older brethren to see who is beginning to fall asleep. There you sit, knowing a big bang is coming, but the sleeper doesn't know it. Then all of a sudden, wham, Dad raps the pulpit and some of those deacons jump pretty high. Dad explains loud and fast for a few minutes while he has their attention.

When he explains to me he doesn't have a Bible or a songbook or a pulpit. So at times I guess I don't get the message. At least I didn't hear him when he told me about the fair. He said, "Junior, I'm sorry we don't have enough money so we can all go to the fair. Since we all can't go, I don't think it would be fair for just one to go, do you?"

Well, I sure didn't think it would be fair for him to give money to one of his kids to go if he couldn't pay for all of us. I guess this wasn't just the way he meant it, but he didn't really explain it. He thought he did, though. Maybe I did forget or maybe I tuned him out.

Anyway, the next afternoon I was just moseying up Main Street looking in on a few places. I watched the sign painter paint a name on the door of a truck. He painted it with yellow then he dusted it with silver with a big powder puff. I saw the guys in the garage wash greasy parts in gasoline. Then I stopped in front of the music store to look at the drums.

While I was standing there Mr. Taylor came out and asked me to do him a favor. He said he wanted to go to the fair but didn't have anyone to go with him. He wanted to know if I'd tag along so he could go.

Of course I went. It wasn't any trouble at all. I couldn't see him missing out going to the fair if my going would fix things up for him.

We had a grand time. The horse races were pretty good. The horses don't run all the time. There is a lot of waiting around. While you are waiting you are supposed to stand on the bottom fence rail, lean over the top fence rail, and then you spit in the dust on the track. This makes you thirsty, so you have to go get a drink of something. Mr. Taylor bought several drinks. He bought ice cream too.

Out in the middle of the track a big gray canvas bag hung over a hole in the ground. There was a wood fire in the hole so the hot air went up into the bag. The longer we watched the bigger the bag got. After a while it was big and round and everybody could tell it was a balloon. From the top there was a rope that came down the side and it had a brickbat tied to the end of it.

There was an announcement about a daredevil making a parachute jump. Then a short, stocky man came out of a tent and walked up to the balloon. Some men fastened a big basket at the bottom of the balloon. Somebody tied a red handkerchief around the man's neck, helped put a big pack of parachutes on his back, and helped him climb into the basket. Next they pulled some slip knots in the ropes holding the whole thing down, and away it went like a bat outa—well, it took off pretty fast.

It went up and up until the man looked very small. Then he jumped out of the basket and out popped a parachute. While he was coming down, the balloon kept going up in a great big arc. The brickbat on the end of the rope kept pulling the top of the balloon down. After the balloon had looked like it was almost flying sideways, its bottom went up and all the hot air whooshed out. The old canvas bag shriveled up like a big prune, then down it came.

By then the man had cut loose his parachute and was falling.

Then out popped another parachute. He didn't ride it very long until he turned it loose like he'd done the first one. He fell a little bit and then the third parachute opened up. He rode it to the ground.

While he was coming down, it looked for the world like the balloon might blow back and hit him. Maybe it would have except he was craning his neck to see where it was. Then he pulled the ropes on the parachute to make it slip to one side and keep away from the balloon.

That balloon came down in a big wad just by the snow cone truck. It didn't hit anybody 'cause they were too busy watching the man to be spending time buying snow cones.

The man came down in an open field back of the grandstand. All those people who paid so much to have a seat for the big event didn't see as good as those of us who were having to run around to keep an eye on everything. Mr. Taylor got all out of breath, but he was able to keep up with me going across the field to where the man came down. For what he'd been through the man looked pretty good. In fact he looked in better shape than Mr. Taylor, who had to go over the barbed wire fence around the field instead of through it like I did.

Then we went back to town. Mr. Taylor thanked me for going along so he could go. And I told him it was no trouble at all and thanked him.

When I got home supper was on the table and everybody else was eating. Of course, Dad wanted to know where I'd been. I told him, "With Mr. Taylor." You can bet his next question was, "Where did Mr. Taylor go?"

About then I began to wonder if I had misunderstood what he meant about if one couldn't go, none of us would. When I told him I'd been to the fair he asked me if he hadn't explained it to me. Then he explained it to me all over again. He really meant that I shouldn't have gone. Then he told me I couldn't have any supper because I was late. That made the rest of the kids happy again. They had looked kind of sad when they heard I'd been to the fair.

After supper Dad explained it to me all over again one more time. I understood it that time. I didn't go back to the fair anymore. And I didn't eat any supper either, and the ice cream had run out a long time ago.

Memo 14: A New Drum

Making plans sure is difficult. I don't mean easy plans for making things like bird houses for purple martins. I mean plans for things you're going to do. These kinds of plans are very difficult if they cover more than one thing or are spread out over very much time.

I didn't think about all the things I should have when I bought my new snare drum.

That drum had been in the music store window for a long time. It was propped up in a corner with the drumsticks crossed in front of it. The carrying strap was sort of folded around behind it. You could see from the sidewalk that the top was made of genuine sheepskin.

Every time I had to go by the music store I just had to stop and have a look at that drum. There was a new drum and bugle corps in town. That must have been what got me interested in the drum.

Anyway, the other day I was standing out there looking and patting my foot like I was marching when Mr. Taylor came out to say hello. I didn't say anything to him about not getting supper because I went to the fair.

He asked me what I had been looking at in his window. I guess he had been watching from inside. I think maybe some storekeepers do that so they can try to sell you something. I told him I looked at a lot of things but most of the time I looked at the drum.

"How would you like to own that drum?" he asked.

Mr. Taylor is a generous man so I had to think about the way he asked that question. If he had said "How would you like to *have* that drum?" it would probably have meant he was going to give it to me. But he said "own" so I figured some sort of a deal was cooking.

"I'd sure like that," I told him.

"I think we can work out something," he went on. "Let's go inside and talk it over." We went in and sat down in his office.

Mr. Taylor told me the drum was on sale for five dollars. Then he asked if I had one dollar. It just so happened that I did. Then he said if I'd give him the dollar he would let me have the drum and I could pay him fifty cents a week for the next eight weeks.

So that's what we agreed on. I gave him the dollar, and he gave me the drum and a card where he can mark off the eight payments.

I strapped on the drum and headed for home. It was all I could do to keep from beating it and marching all the way. I ran most of the way, so I couldn't take time to beat it anyhow. I had to be careful not to trip and fall on my new drum.

Mom was sure surprised. She asked me all kinds of questions. Mostly I think she wanted to be sure I hadn't stolen anything. Finally she said it was OK to keep the drum and to be sure and pay Mr. Taylor the first thing every payday.

Soon it began to dawn on me that eight weeks is a long time. Fifty cents didn't seem like much sitting in Mr. Taylor's office. Thinking about leaving the store after work each week and stopping at his place and giving him a whole half dollar began to seem like a lot to give up just to have a drum. And what would I do if I lost my job?

Things didn't work out so well the evening the drum and bugle corps practiced either. When they lined up out in the street, I got all set to go up on the sidewalk. Some of those big guys looked over and grinned, so I thought everything was fine. So when they started marching, I started too. I'd been practicing in the backyard and had it down pat. Mom wouldn't let me practice in the house. She said five kids was bad enough—five kids and a drum was too much. She said to practice in the coal shed. There wasn't room enough for marching in there, so I practiced all around the garden and up and down the path to the old outhouse we don't use 'cause we've got a bathroom at this place.

Me and the drum and bugle corps covered about a half block before some of the guys got to laughing instead of grinning. The drum major blew his whistle so everything came to a halt. He yelled, "All right, you guys, cut out the monkey business and keep in time." The bugles hadn't blowed anything yet.

We got started again but only made it for another half block before we stopped. The drum major couldn't get the bugles to get started together so he blew his whistle again.

This time he came over and said, "That's a nice looking drum you got there."

I thanked him.

He said, "Those red rings around it don't look as good as the mahogany on our drums."

Up until then I'd thought they were pretty fancy.

"The tone is different too," he said. "Your drum isn't as big from top to bottom as ours."

He was right there.

"You see, it sounds different. Sort of kid stuff, so why don't you practice somewhere else? And before you say it, I know this is a public sidewalk. So I'm just asking you to go someplace else. I'm not telling you to."

I didn't figure on going, even if my drum really didn't look so good as those bigger ones. That was the truth, but it made me feel sort of bad.

Finally the drum major had a great idea. He said I could ride his new streamlined bike that was parked over by the junior high gym. He needed somebody to watch it for him, anyhow.

I said OK and walked off toward the gym. The bike was pretty big, though, and I couldn't ride it and hold the drum and sticks. I was afraid I'd bust the drum. I didn't want to do that 'cause it was still a pretty good drum even if it was little and had red stripes.

There was nothing to do but run home, leave the drum, and hurry back to the bike. When I got back some bigger kid was riding the bike and the drum and bugle corps was about five blocks way up the street.

There I stood with my hands in my pockets. No bike. No playing the drum on the sidewalk. Just fifty cents a week to pay at the music store. Things sure weren't the way I planned them.

To make things worse I got a job with the town boy's band the next week. It wasn't with my snare drum, though. They had enough of them, which is another thing I forgot to check on before I bought my snare drum.

I was just standing around in the Legion Hall waiting for practice to start when Mr. Lewis asked me if I could beat a drum. Naturally I told him I could. Then he gave me the big padded stick and told me his regular bass drummer had moved out of town. He said to watch his baton and every time it came down for me to hit the drum. When his left hand went palm up, I was to hit the drum hard. When he turned palm down, I was to hit it easy.

So now I'm in the band. The bass drum is furnished. I don't

need the snare drum, but I've still got those payments to make. Mom says I can't go back on my word. That's especially bad for preacher's kids to do. Things sure aren't like I planned them.

Memo 15: The Catholic Social

Boy, if you don't pay any attention to anything else, you'd better listen to this. Baptist preacher's kids don't play in the band at Catholic ice cream socials. If you ever pull that trick, your hide won't hold shucks. I just made that mistake and there is heck to pay. Some of those old women up at Cobden say it's horrible what I did. They are even thinking of not paying anything to associational missions because the missionary's kid is "helping that other denomination in their endeavors."

It's too bad that things had to happen that way because we are having great fun in Cy Lewis' band. We are still practicing every week over at the Legion Hall. It's really not a hall. It's a big, old, white frame house that has an enormous living room and the dining room is next to it. A wide door connects the two rooms. The clarinets and trumpets are in the living room. I'm at the back of the dining room behind the trombones, alto horns, and the tuba.

One of our favorite pieces is "Over the Waves." Some people think its smart to talk about that being our theme song 'cause we are all wet. But we have a good time playing it. In the living room the clarinets play the melody most of the time. In case you don't know, "Over the Waves" is in three-quarter time. Its really a waltz, but a waltz is a dance and Dad says dancing is wicked and to call it three-quarter time.

Anyway, back in the dining room on the first beat I *boom* the bass drum. The snare drums and the trombones *pa-pa* the last two beats. We get such a loud *boom, pa-pa* going that sometimes we can't hear the melody. That's when Cy raises his eyebrows and turns his palm down. Then he looks at the front rows and turns his palm up again. Its a good thing its summer and the windows are open. We'd have trouble if all that music had to stay in the house. The way it is the neighbors get a free concert.

We were going to give a concert last Friday night. Cy told us to wear our white shirt and pants and a black tie. We got to the Legion Hall early and loaded everything into his Model T touring coupe. It has a rumble seat in back. The door opens up and back so the bass drum just fits right in there. We piled the other instruments around the drum and on top of the car. We had to be careful and not tear the rag top. Some kids crowded onto the seat with Cy, and the rest of us got on the running boards, fenders, and bumpers. Cy drove slowly, and we made it the five miles up to Cobden with no trouble. Some kids went in another car but didn't have near the fun we did.

I never had a second thought about religion when he drove up to the Catholic Church. They had a lot of freezers of homemade ice cream and a package or two of the store-bought kind. There was a pyramid of soda pop in cases and a water trough full of soda in ice water. The women were cooking hamburgers and hot dogs to go in a white mountain of buns. The catsup and mustard were in gallon jars. Those Catholics may be stingy with the water for baptizing, but they don't skimp when it comes to food.

Right off we were given tickets worth a nickel apiece—a whole quarter—before we'd even played a note. But we couldn't buy anything until the intermission. Sandwiches and drinks and cones were only five cents each for the band boys. We got pretty hungry just thinking ahead to the first intermission, so you can bet we started playing right away. We played loud too. Its a good thing we were outside. When we finished a piece everybody who wasn't holding a sandwich clapped. That made us play louder on the next tune, but Cy wasn't turning his palm down very often anyway. In fact, he was up there waving his baton, patting his foot, and grinning like he was thinking of food too.

There was a big crowd. Everybody was really enjoying themselves. I knew a lot of people from over at the Baptist church, and there were even people from some of the country churches where Dad has preached. The way they lit into those hamburgers and hot dogs they weren't worrying a bit about a social not being the right way to finance a church.

When the crowd began to thin out, we didn't play so loud or so often. We didn't have any more intermissions either. That didn't make much difference 'cause by then we were all out of tickets.

There were a few people still hanging around when Cy said to pack up and get ready to go. It didn't take long to pack so we got to looking around. There were a few bottles of pop in the bottom of the trough. Some of the ladies said we could help ourselves 'cause it would just go to waste if we didn't drink it. The bottle I got must have been overlooked for a long time. It was the coldest one I'd had all night. There was still some more ice cream in the bottom of the freezers. We had to drink some of it we couldn't get on a spoon.

I was just finishing that last bottle of pop and was trying to wipe the vanilla ice cream dribbles off my black tie when one of the women from Second Baptist walked up. The people from that church split off from First Baptist long before Dad preached there, but they still hadn't forgotten how mad they had been when they split.

The woman said, "Aren't you Junior, the missionary's kid?"

I told her, "Yep, I sure am."

Then she asked, "Well, what are you doing here?"

"Playing in the band." I thought she ought to be able to see that for herself. I had on that white outfit and the drumstick was stuck in my belt.

"I was afraid of that," she said. "Some people just don't pay any attention to where their children go these days."

I didn't spend much time thinking about her last remark. When I got home, Dad asked where we played and I told him, "Up at Cobden at one of the churches."

"Which one?"

I didn't see that it made much difference, but I said, "Catholic."

Dad just raised his eyebrows and said, "Oh?"

I thought that was the end of it until Dad went over to Jonesboro at the end of the month to get paid. The treasurer showed him the letter he got from some lady up in Cobden.

Dad seemed worried about the whole thing for several days. I thought the treasurer had the right idea. He said, "Think nothing of it, Brother Smith. They don't give anything, nohow."

Now when we play, I have to ask Cy ahead of time where we are going to play and who we are playing for.

I don't want to stir up more trouble for Dad since I'm moving up in the band. I'm trading my snare drum and two dollars to Mr. Taylor for a trombone. The new kid can have the *booms* on the bass drum. I'm going to go after those *pa-pas* when we play "Over the Waves" and other wal—three-quarter time pieces.

Memo 16: The Library

There are some more things you should know about the library. It is a very valuable place. When Dad is studying and I just can't keep quiet enough, I go to the library. And I can't always learn enough from schoolbooks so I find what the subject is and go read about it in library books. Sometimes that gives me a problem 'cause all those books don't always say the same things about the same subject.

A lot of fellows and some girls go to our library. It is a low stone building that is very easy to climb on the outside. If it's too crowded on the inside, like on Monday nights, we climb on the outside and get books handed to us through the window.

Monday is the crowded night because that's when we read the Sunday funnies. The library gets a lot of big city papers, especially from Saint Louis and Chicago. Some of them have some of the same comics so we have to keep passing them around until we have read all of them.

Magazines are the favorite reading for some kids. I like to read some of them about radios and science. Mostly I have to get the very old copies so I can cut them up. The librarian saves them for me 'cause she knows we can't afford magazines at our house. The schoolteachers keep giving us work making notebooks in geography and history. We have to have pictures for the notebooks, and it is tough for some of us who do not have magazines. Teachers should miss a few paychecks like preachers do so they would quit having kids make notebooks that have to have pictures in them.

Old *Radio Craft* magazines are stacked in the back room of the library. I like to read them because they can be checked out longer than the new ones. Sometimes after I check out a magazine, I go back and trade it for one I like better. That way the one I've checked out is still there and I can keep the one I've traded for. Dad would surely tan my hide if he knew about that.

Medical books are in one part of the library. They are marked for adults only, but sometimes the librarian is busy and some librarians don't care if kids read them. Sometimes when we finish the funnies one of the fellows will say, "Hey, Smitty, Miss Blank is working tonight, let's go look at the doctor book." So we go look at the pictures and read how babies are born. If you read it at the library, its not like it is in dirty books. The doctors who write books know more good stuff than the people who write dirty books.

When you get old enough to go to the library be sure to see how many sections have information about the same man. You can learn a lot more that way. What I mean is like—well, take Benjamin Franklin, for instance. He is in the history book. That is kind of a dry book, but in there it says he was a printer and a scientist.

Next you look in the encyclopedia under printing. That's a lot more fun and it tells more about Franklin. Then you look in the science books and you learn more about printing and something about electricity. You also find out about politics along with printing. That takes you back to the history books but also to more interesting books.

Some of the guys try to get the girls to look at the art books with them. Most of the girls won't do it though. They know the fellows are going to turn to pictures of statues. Not all of the old artists knew how to chisel fig leaves. Most of the women statues are too fat. The corset and brassiere sections of the Sears and Roebuck catalogs have better pictures.

Mr. Johnson is my favorite junior high school teacher. He has always been nice to me. He has been extra nice since we took some special tests.

A few weeks after those tests, he read the honor roll and I didn't make it again. Sometimes I'm on it and sometimes I'm not. Once in the fifth grade and once in the sixth grade I got put back in the *B* class. I didn't like it there so I paid attention the next month and got back into the *A* class. I can stay there if I want to, but sometimes things aren't so interesting.

After he read the honor roll, Mr. Johnson waited awhile and came back to talk to me. He said, "Why aren't you on the honor roll, David?"

"I don't know."

"Don't you know I think you could be on there if you tried to be?"

"Oh, I could be on there if I tried." I didn't think I was bragging, 'cause I really thought I could.

"Do you remember those special tests we gave you?"

"Yes."

"On that battery of test you scored equal to the ninth year of school plus several months. That's like a sophomore in high school, but don't get bigheaded about it."

"I won't" I told him, but to tell the truth I was feeling pretty good. Feeling like I do sometimes just before I get into trouble.

"Tell me why you think you do not do as well in school, David."

"Well, I haven't got all my books yet."

"Why don't you have them?" he wanted to know.

"Because my daddy is a preacher and he don't—doesn't—always get paid when he preaches, so I can't ask him to buy me books. Besides my littler sisters need books worse than I do 'cause they can't go to the library after dark."

"Go to the library?" He was looking at me very closely.

"Yes. There are books there just like our schoolbooks. Sometimes they are the same ones. I go up there to do my studying. Sometimes I get sidetracked if I find something more interesting than our lessons."

"Do you read biographies?" he asked.

"Yes."

"Science, electricity?"

"Yes."

"How about doctor books? Do you read them?"

My face felt sort of warm, but I admitted I did.

"Well, that explains it," he said and grinned as he gave me a slap on the shoulder.

"Explains what? How did you know what I read?" I wanted to know. He didn't just happen to ask all those right questions.

"Those were pretty good tests, David. They told me you studied a lot more than what we have in class, and they told me what you study."

I was glad they did if that made him come talk to me like he did. He sat looking at me for a while like he was thinking about what to say.

"You'd better keep the test results to yourself," he suggested.

"I will. Thank you."

"And try to study the assignments even if they are not always as interesting as the other things you read about. They are necessary things that you should know."

"I'll try," I promised.

He was a very nice man. He had a Chevrolet coupe with a gear shift and he took me in it to see the gravel pit, the dairy at the state hospital, and a gas-electric train over on the M & O railroad. He also gave me used copies of the books I needed for class and some extra books he thought would be interesting. They usually were.

I guess the main things for you to remember about the library are that it gets you out of the house when Dad is studying, and it can help with the tests at school.

You're going to learn that preachers study a lot so they can help other people. That gives you time to go to the library to study things for yourself. If you study a lot of big things real hard maybe some other man who has a car will give you books and take you to interesting places.

Maybe if I can help Dad get a car in a few years, he can take us to interesting places when you are bigger. Right now he only goes to church and weddings and funerals. But that works out OK 'cause people take him to their church in their car. They have most of the weddings at our house, and he rides to the funerals in the hearse.

Memo 17: Don't Throw Rocks

Preacher's kids have to learn to throw dirt clods instead of rocks. Breaking windows, denting cars, hitting the side of a house, and hurting people are all worse if done with a rock instead of a clod. They seem to be worse if done by a PK instead of some other kid. A preacher's kid with a rock for throwing is sure headed for trouble unless he's just skipping flat rocks across a pond. Even then he'd better take a good look to see that everything is in the clear on the other side.

Dad's private sermon to me about rock throwing goes something like this. "Don't throw rocks. But if you just have to throw something, throw a ball. Be careful doing that. Don't hit anyone. And when you throw at Treece's chickens in our garden, throw dirt clods—small ones."

Those chickens are what stirs up trouble. Every morning they come strutting across the road and make a beeline for the tomato patch. I chase them out of there before they can eat the ripe tomatoes or peck holes in the big green ones. Then they scratch the dirt away from the peanut ridges. That dirt has to stay in the ridge cause the peanuts are growing in there. So I run them out of there and they go to whatever is just coming through the ground and start scratching it up.

The old rooster is the worst of the whole bunch. He struts around, bossing the hens and the half-grown chickens. He fertilizes the hen's eggs, but I'm not supposed to watch that. He has sharp spurs on his heels that can cut or scratch. Since I can't get too close to him, I have to throw something at him—dirt clods.

Dad says, "Be careful of that old rooster. He can flog you and hurt you, but don't you hurt him. Throw at him real easy."

This morning I looked out front and there was the whole passel of chickens coming across the road. Old Pappy Treece was sitting on his front porch watching them, but he wasn't about to call them back.

First the chickens milled around the front flower bed just eating bugs and worms. That's good for the flowers. Guess the blossoms don't taste good enough to eat. Pappy was watching them, and he was watching me, and I was watching both him and the chickens.

The next thing I knew those chickens started picking their way through the flowers alongside the house. Pappy and me both knew they were heading for our garden. He didn't do anything to stop them, so I had to get busy.

I ran out to the back of the garden and picked the tomatoes. It was earlier than I had intended to pick them, but they had to be taken out of the way of those chickens.

When I finished picking and started toward the house, that old rooster was just leading his gang into the lettuce bed. Just seeing him marching in there made me so mad I started looking for a clod to throw at him.

The only thing I could find quickly sure looked like a clod. It just could have been a rock with dirt on it. The way it didn't break into pieces when it hit sort of makes me wonder if it was really and truly a clod. Anyway, I didn't use up a whole lot of time inspecting that rock—clod.

I set the tomato basket down, took a pretty careful aim, and let her fly low and flat just off the ground and just over the potato plants. I'll bet a lot of potato bugs had heart failure when that chunk went by them.

Old rooster rared up to see what was coming. He flapped his wings for a fast start and headed for home. The hens turned tail to go with him. Most of the fryers decided they'd join in for the trip back across the road. One big, old, gray fryer didn't make it. He sort of stretched up and stuck his neck right in front of the clod that just missed the rooster.

Have you ever seen a chicken with a U-shaped neck? He doesn't look very good and he acts even worse. That old boy flopped over and for a while he jerked around just like a chicken with his head wrung off. Then he quit jerking and laid still, very still.

There wasn't a thing I could do but pick him up and take him home. He wasn't going to make it under his own steam.

Pappy was still sitting on the porch. He saw me coming, holding that fryer by his feet, his beak almost touching the ground. Pappy didn't get up or say anything. I put the chicken down in the edge of his yard next to the pool with the big goldfish in it.

I sure hope Pappy was figuring on having fried chicken for lunch. I noticed he didn't let it lay there long. He keeps his chickens penned up now, and Dad is still not convinced that rock was a clod.

Memo 18: People Die

Our family is one of the first to learn when someone dies. Many times we know somebody is about to die so Dad can be there when it happens. He prays for the person who is very sick or hurt. He prays for his mother and dad, brothers and sisters, or anyone who is going to feel real sorry because he died.

Being with sick or dying people is a tough part of Dad's job as a preacher. He is supposed to help people, and I think he and God do make some of them feel better. Maybe not right away, but later on when they think about it for a while.

If the people feel as much better as Dad feels worse, then he must help them. Sometimes when he comes home from visiting at a home or a hospital, he goes into his bedroom and shuts the door. He doesn't come out for a long time. When he does come out he is very tired and crabby and doesn't eat very well.

Preachers' kids see more people die than other people's kids do. Take the other night when old Mr. Harper died, for instance. Betty and me were the only kids there. I would rather have been someplace else, especially since I liked Mr. Harper, and Dad prayed real hard for him.

Mr. Harper lived just across the alley from us. He didn't work at a regular job. He was what they call *retired*. That means he had worked a long time and had enough money to live on by having his daughter, her husband, and her kids live with him to keep expenses down.

He worked around the house a lot, kept the yard looking real good, but he didn't yell at kids who cut across it on the way to school. Also, he had time to pick apples and strawberries which he shared with our family.

Mr. Harper stood very tall until he began to feel bad. Then he started to stoop over when he walked. He used to help his son-in-law start the car on cold mornings by holding the choke and working the spark lever. He showed me how they worked, so I could work them some of the time. He was my friend.

Then Mr. Harper got sick. We didn't see him outside very much. His yard began to get kind of cruddy. Then he had to go to bed and probably would never get up again.

Dad began to visit him almost every day to try to cheer him

up. He prayed for him to get well. He didn't have to pray for him to get saved 'cause Mr. Harper and Dad and everybody figured he was going to heaven. He said, "I settled that years ago when I was a lad, Preacher."

The other night when we were about ready to go to bed, there was a loud banging at the back door. Dad opened it and said, "Good evening, Harry, what can we do for you?" I looked around Dad and there stood Harry. He's a little older and bigger than me, and he was all white-faced with his eyes bugging out. He was breathing hard and looked very scared—more scared than he would be just from running across the alley in the dark.

"It's Grandpa, Brother Smith. The doctor's there and he says he's going fast. You'd better hurry."

"I'm going to the Harper's, Grace. You'd better come as soon as you can." Then Dad ran out into the dark.

Mom didn't have anyone to leave us with so she took us by the hand and we followed Dad. It was the first time in a long time I went to a member's house without getting my hands and face washed and my hair combed.

As we went into Harper's backyard we could hear Harry's momma carrying on. She was sort of moaning and yelling. When she said anything it was mostly, "O Lord, what are we going to do?" and "Please God, don't take him, but don't let him suffer." The way I'd seen him stooped over and hurting, it seemed to me she needed to make up her mind. Even I could tell if he stayed here he was suffering and heaven should be a lot better.

The lights were all on in the Harper's house, just bare bulbs hanging from the middle of the ceiling by a long wire. We went through the kitchen to the dining room then through a side door into the bedroom where Mr. Harper was. He looked very thin and gray. The light bulb had a shade and a cloth over it so it wouldn't shine in his eyes. But he couldn't see anyhow 'cause his eyes were closed. He wasn't breathing deeply much, but his breathing was sort of fast. He'd swallow once in a while and his Adam's apple would go way up and make a dry sound come out of his mouth.

Old Mrs. Harper was just sitting very still and looking at him. Mom put her hand on the old lady's shoulder, and Mrs. Harper reached up and put her hand on Mom's. Both of them had tears running slowly down into the corners of their mouths.

Dad was holding one of Mr. Harper's hands and rubbing his wrist.

He'd rub from the hand toward the upper part of his arm. He lowered his head like he was praying part of the time, but he kept rubbing. "Should I keep rubbing, Doctor?" he asked once, more to break the quiet than anything else, I thought.

"Might as well. Won't hurt a thing," old Doc said and kept listening with that thing he had plugged into his ears.

Mr. Harper kept breathing faster and faster but not very deep. Then he started breathing a lot slower. Doc leaned over and pushed the hearing thing down harder on Mr. Harper's chest. Then Mr. Harper took a long breath in, and then it sort of came back out long and easy like by itself with him not helping push it out at all. Doc turned his head sidewise and lifted one of Mr. Harper's eyelids up. I couldn't see in that eye, but I was afraid I didn't want to anyway. Doc turned the eyelid loose and pushed it back closed with his forefinger.

He looked across the bed at old Mrs. Harper. "He's gone. I'm sorry," he said.

Mrs. Harper just sat there for a long time. Nobody said anything. She leaned over and patted Mr. Harper's hand that Dad had been holding. Then she walked out of the room. Doc pulled the sheet up over Mr. Harper's head and the rest of us left the room. Mrs. Harper was in the kitchen fixing coffee already.

"Won't you folks sit a spell and have a cup of coffee with me? You want the children to have some milk and cookies, Sister Smith?"

Mom said that would be fine, so we all sat down. My stomach was cutting up a little, but I figured a little bite would settle it down.

Harry's momma put her elbows on the table and then put her face into her hands. She started to moan again. Mrs. Harper said, "You may as well hush, Mary. Dad can't hear you now, and the Lord's will has been done. He's already in heaven and happy. That's just his old tired body in there in the bedroom." Then she sat down and started crying softly.

Mom poured coffee for Mrs. Harper and anybody else who wanted a cup. We got our milk and cookies. Dad went around shaking hands and talking very low to everyone in the family.

We hadn't been there very long before a neighbor lady came in with a big enameled coffeepot full of hot tea. Somebody brought a dishpan of cookies, somebody brought slaw, and a big ham was handed through the kitchen door. It was like everybody knew when

Mr. Harper was going to die and had the food for the family all ready.

Later someone said the undertaker was out front, so Mom said, "Come on, children, we'd better go."

I didn't sleep too good that night. The next day Harry said the undertaker didn't do like people said he would: put a mirror up to his grandpa's mouth and pennies on his eyes. At least the undertaker didn't before they took Mr. Harper's body away.

If seeing people die is something special preacher's kids get to see, I'd just as soon do without it. It makes me feel about the same way if we find out we are going to have to move again.

Memo 19: Pigeon-toed Thief

It's funny how preacher's kids learn to take a close look at people. I guess we get into the habit of looking at them so we can see if all the things we hear about church members are true. When the pastor is asked to pray for some member's kid who has the chicken pox, it's only natural for us to see if the pox left scars when the kid gets back to church.

The habit of looking caused me to notice that Mr. Jackson, the school superintendent, was pigeon-toed. Noticing that wasn't really anything to be proud of observing 'cause he was pigeon-toed enough that it really didn't take a very close look.

There were times when I thought it might be handy to be a little bit pigeon-toed. It would sure help a fellow climb up the corner of the junior high school.

The schoolhouse is just across the street from our place. We play on the high bars, tennis courts, giant strides, and we climb the fire escapes and the building. Half of the basement is above ground so there is a stone ledge about five feet up all around the school. At any outside corner we can find toeholds, climb to the ledge, then walk on it all the way around the building.

Once on the ledge we can slip fingers and toes on the bricks at the corners and climb to the second story. The corner bricks are laid one sticking out and the other sunken in, almost like steps. Being pigeon-toed would help climb those corners.

One night there was a carnival held in the gymnasium. A lot of people were there. I didn't have a very good time because I didn't have much spending money, and there were no paying jobs. Cakes and pies, cookies and rag dolls—everything—were donated, so naturally kids weren't paid for doing anything.

The next day some of us went over to see if there were anything good left over. We didn't find anything worth much so we decided to climb the schoolhouse. We started on the back side 'cause there were a lot of cars including the sheriff's out front. Everything went OK until we walked the ledge past the open window of the school office.

I got there first and sure was startled when the sheriff himself looked up and said, "What you doin' there, Kid?"

"Nothin'. Just walkin' the ledge and lookin'."

"You're the preacher's kid, aren't you?" he asked.

"Yep." Seems like everybody knows the PKs so there ain't—isn't— much use trying to hide it or lie about it.

Just when I thought he'd tell me to go away all he said was, "Well, you be careful and don't fall from there, and don't you even think about climbing in that window."

Well now, I wasn't going to do that. There was such a mess in that office. There was white powdery stuff all over the floor. If I'd got that on my clothes Mom would've had a fit. So I just stood on the ledge and kept looking in.

Pretty soon the sheriff closed the door of the big, old safe and I could see a big hole in the safe door that had let all that white stuff spill out. The door was metal on both sides and all around the edges and was filled with white caked stuff. It looked like wet flour, but I knew it wasn't.

"What's all that white junk," I asked.

"That's asbestos," the sheriff replied.

"Sure made a mess."

"You can say that again."

I was looking at the dirty floor when I noticed a set of foot tracks going out of the office door into the hallway. They were just as plain as could be on that oiled pine floor, and they were sure pigeon-toed tracks.

"You know who is pigeon-toed around here, Sheriff?" I asked. The sheriff started laughing and looked up at me. Then he sat down in the superintendent's chair and really had a good laugh.

Finally he said, "You're pretty observant, kid, but don't get any big ideas."

About that time Mr. Jackson came into the office, and I figured it was time to leave, but the sheriff said, "What'd you just say a minute ago, Smitty?"

I wasn't about to talk up right then, so he asked again, "What did you say about those tracks?"

"I didn't say nothin' about those tracks," I told him truthfully. "I just asked you a question."

"Yeah, that's right," the sheriff said. "He thinks the thief was pigeon-toed, Jackson. Ain't that a laugh?"

I didn't stay around to see if Mr. Jackson thought it was funny or not. I dropped off the ledge and skedaddled home. The other kids saw me running and they took off too.

Things turned out good and bad after that. Signs were put up saying not to climb the schoolhouse. The carnival money was found and returned. I didn't get my perfect attendance certificate signed by the superintendent of schools. And now the sheriff waves at me when we see each other.

Memo 20: Doc Tweedy

"Study to show thyself approved unto God, a workman that needeth not to be ashamed" (2 Tim. 2:15).

That is a verse we had to learn in church. It came to mind today because we are moving back to Cobden. That is where Doctor Tweedy lives. He used to be our doctor. He is a friend of Mom's and Dad's and I like him a lot.

Before I ever went to school we lived in Cobden, just down the street from Doc. He had a big Veely car that was powerful enough to go over the steep, rough hills of Union County.

Mrs. Tweedy had a new Model A Ford. The first day she got it she took Mom and me for a ride. It had the first gear shift I had even seen. Since it was a coupe I got to stand up and look right straight out the windshield. We sure went fast. Most people were like us and couldn't afford cars. They stopped to see who was riding in the new car.

Doc had the only radio I saw for a long time. It had a big crooked horn that the sound came out of. One night he told me, "Junior, reach down in that horn and feel the little man who is talking." I stood on tiptoe and stuck my arm down in the horn. That thing let out an awful squeal so I got my arm out of there in a hurry.

Doc said, "What happened? Did you pinch him and make him squeal?"

I told him, "Nope" and reached in again. That thing squealed again but that time I saw Doc twisting one of the radio knobs and knew he was just fooling me.

He and Dad had a good laugh. Doc said, "Brother Hosea, he sure wasn't afraid to stick his hand back down there to find out what was going on."

That made me feel a little better about being tricked. That radio was a very interesting piece of equipment.

Doc does a lot at the church. He teaches a men's class. He is a deacon and he leads the singing. Mrs. Tweedy plays the piano part of the time. Mom plays it some too.

Doc has a deep voice. It's easy to listen to, and he has a gold tooth that sometimes sparkles when he sings. His hair sort of falls down across his forehead on loud, fast songs. He just swats it back in place on the upbeat and keeps on marking time with his right hand.

There are times when Doc has to leave church right in the middle of the singing, the sermon, or whatever is going on. Somebody comes across the street from his house and sticks his head in the doorway. If Doc doesn't see him, somebody else gives him a nudge and away he goes. All this means that somebody is sick or hurt or is going to have a baby.

When I grow up I hope my job is important enough for people to call me out of church.

Doc always wears a big, red fountain pen in his coat pocket. He uses that pen to write on a piece of paper the name of medicines that will make people get well. If Doc doesn't give people the pills, he gives them the paper to take to the drugstore. Then the druggist gives them the medicine. All the names are written in Latin. Doc must be awful smart, and that pen writes in two languages.

When people get sick at night, Doc has to get on some clothes, start his car, and take off. There are times when he has been gone for a while and somebody comes for Dad. Then we know the person is very sick.

If people who are Doc's patients die, he is very sad. Dad preaches the funeral, but Doc doesn't sing with the choir. He sits with the people close to the family, and sometimes he cries like it was one of his family. Dad rides to the cemetery in the hearse, but Doc brings him home.

One day Dad's elastic exerciser slipped off of his foot and cut a big gash over Betty's eye. Doc came running to our house to fix her eye. He had Mom and Dad hold Betty on the kitchen table while he washed her face and head. I pumped water from the cistern pump on the back porch and carried I don't know how many bucketfuls to the kitchen.

Doc got the place sewed up and gave Betty something to put her to sleep. Then he said, "Well, between the two of us we got her fixed up, Junior Boy." He didn't have to say that 'cause he really did most of the work. It made me feel good that he did, though.

So we are moving back to Cobden, and I'll see my friend Doc more often. The reason I thought of that Scripture is that I think Doc is a workman approved unto God. He hasn't got anything to be ashamed of that I know about.

I know that Dad says we should use Jesus as our example and try to be like him. Just the same, Doc seems a whole lot closer than Jesus, so I study what he does. Somehow I think if boys my age try to be like Doc, we will be more like Jesus and he will understand.

Memo 21: Dad Got Arrested

Some day you are going to hear about Dad getting arrested, so I want to tell you just what happened. A few people know the true story, but a lot of others are just guessing or just gossiping.

Dad just doesn't know what to do or say about it. Mostly he just keeps still and worries. He didn't have to go to jail, but the sheriff did pick him up in front of a lot of people on the front steps of the Anna Church.

It's kind of a long story so I'll start way back when Mom and Dad were first married. In between terms in the seminary at New Orleans, the old Baptist Bible Institute, they came to Cobden for a short time. They stayed with a nice older lady. I'll just call her Grandma. She owned the house we live in now, and she was just like a mother to Mom and Dad. Mom talks a lot about the good times they all had. They ate a lot of cantaloupes with ice cream in them, for one thing.

When we moved back this time we were all very happy to live in the big old house where Mom was happy before. But things aren't the same. Mr. Sam, Grandma's son, looks after the property now. He is the landlord, and he wants everybody to know it. He hangs around the house and his other property near us all the time. He never likes anything that is going on. Mostly it is none of his business 'cause we won't hurt the property. Now the place is cleaner and better fixed up than when we moved into it.

Anyway, we have been having a hard time paying the rent, so Dad asked Mr. Sam if there was some work to be done for part of the rent. The way I see it, Mr. Sam owed Dad something for work he'd already done. Mr. Sam said he had a big job coming up and could give Dad a lot of work.

In a few days Dad and Mr. Sam and some other men started getting up early and going up to Herrin to move a house down to Cobden. Up there a lot of the coal mines had shut down, putting many men out of work. Some towns had plenty of empty houses 'cause people moved away. Those empty houses sold cheap, so Mr. Sam bought one.

Dad and the other men cut the house in two so it could be loaded onto a truck. Then they hauled it to Cobden and put it on a new foundation they had poured on a vacant lot across the creek from our yard. They put the halves together and patched the roofing and the siding. Dad is a good painter so the old house was soon looking pretty good in its new location.

Almost every night Dad and Mr. Sam would talk awhile after everyone else was gone. Mr. Sam knew we lived right there, so he'd ask Dad to do some little extra things or finish up something after supper.

When Saturday came none of the others worked on the place, but Dad always seemed to have something to do. It got so he had to rush to get finished and off to his weekend preaching.

You see, with us having no car somebody has to come for Dad. Or he has to ride the train sometimes and catch a ride part of the way. Sometimes he just has to thumb a ride or start walking.

I feel bad when he has to thumb. The hard road goes by our place and I would like to stand there with him until he gets a ride. But people wouldn't take a man and a boy. So I sit on the front step and pretend to be reading until I see a car stop for him. It's tough to be associational missionary without a car, but you can't afford a car on a missionary's salary—especially when they don't pay it regularly.

Mr. Sam just had no idea how much time Dad was working for him. When they added it all up he didn't believe Dad, and I know Dad didn't even keep track of some of his time.

Mr. Sam said he couldn't allow on the rent for all that time. He said he and Grandma had to have something coming in for rent to live on. Dad said we didn't have to have all of his work allowed on one month. He'd pay some rent and carry the allowance over on some other months. Sam said he'd carry over some of it, but he still didn't think he'd pay for all the time Dad turned in.

The upshot of it all was that after a few months Mr. Sam said we owed some rent. Dad said he hadn't got any money or allowance for all his work. Then Mr. Sam said he was going to sue us to get his rent. I think Dad tried to borrow money at the bank to pay what Mr. Sam said we owed. I'm just guessing, but I think Dad's friend at the bank said, "Brother Smith, if you don't owe it, don't pay it." So Dad didn't pay.

I didn't hear anymore about it for a long time. People rented the house that was put back together, and Mr. Sam started pestering them and quit bothering us. Just before associational meeting time Mr. Sam wanted a garage built from some leftover lumber, but Dad said he was too busy to help.

Then Dad went to the associational meeting. On the second day he was standing on the front steps talking to friends when the sheriff came up to him. He said, "Are you Reverend Smith?"

Dad said he was.

Then the sheriff took a paper out of his pocket and said, "I've got a summons for you for not paying your debts. You'll have to go to the courthouse with me."

Dad didn't even know what it was all about. He was terribly embarrassed right there in public. They had to get a clerk pro tem to go ahead with the meeting. Dad went with the sheriff to Jonesboro to find out what was going on. When he got there, he had to go to see Mr. Sam's lawyer because Mr. Sam was suing for the rent he said Dad owed.

Before it was all over someone offered to help Dad. They pointed out that it was Grandma's house not Mr. Sam's. If anybody sued Dad, it should be Grandma, so they went to see her.

The first thing she said was, "Why, Brother Smith, I'm so glad to see you. It's so nice of you to come visit me. Come in and have a chair."

Then Dad told her about Mr. Sam and the lawsuit, and Grandma began to cry. She just kept telling Dad over and over how sorry she was. Then she called up that lawyer and told him what for. I don't know what she told Mr. Sam. But Dad didn't have to go to jail, and Mr. Sam never bothered us anymore.

We have a nice place to live. It is a big house that sets up on a hill looking down on the highway and across to the Illinois Central Railroad. Freight trains with big black engines go by and the engineers and firemen wave at us. The *Panama Limited* streaks past with its whistle screaming.

In the wintertime snow makes our hill good for sledding. There is an interesting old barn to play in down close to the other house. The creek has perch I can catch on a bent pin with just a white paper wad or a grasshopper for bait. When the water runs fast I make boats of different shapes and pull them with a pole and string. There is even an old pear orchard out back that still has lots of good pears in it for eating and for preserves.

It is really a good place for our family. Mom and Dad are generally happy. Dad's work is getting better. As long as Grandma stays alive we will be all right. But if Mr. Sam ever has his way, I'll bet he tries to pull something on Dad again.

But Dad just says, "Remember to do unto others as you would have them do unto you." Then he treats Mr. Sam as nice as he can, but I tell you, I'm having trouble keeping from throwing rocks at his car.

Memo 22: The Medicine Show

There are many things that are normal for other kids to do, but for some reason they are wrong when preacher's kids do them. At least, people call Mom and Dad and tell on us for doing them.

Going to picture shows is probably the worst thing. It's especially bad if you go on Sunday afternoon or prayer meeting night. Going to a church of another denomination is not very good either. Playing ball or fishing on Sunday is also bad. I once went crawdad trapping with tin cans in the creek on Sunday afternoon and didn't get reported. That probably would have been bad, too, if I'd got caught. Couldn't even bring the crawdads home.

Last night I found out that going to a medicine show is about the most awful thing a preacher's son can do. It was especially bad since Dad was out of town, and it caused Mom a lot of trouble.

It all started when Arnie asked me to his house to play ante over. Arnie lives across the creek and over on the other side of the cornfield. Mom said it was all right if I went but not to stay too late.

We had been playing for a long time when we first heard the music. It was just getting dark so we were already having trouble seeing the ball come over the house. We slowed down playing, and that's when the music came through pretty loud.

"What's that music?" Arnie wanted to know. "Don't sound like no band."

Now, since I've played the trombone and beat the drums in a band, I was sure it wasn't a band.

"You're right. That ain't no band. It's not an orchestra either, no violins."

"Maybe we'd better check it out," Arnie suggested. "Don't sound very far away."

Somehow I didn't think it would take long, so I never thought to run home and tell Mom we were going checking on the music. We just started wandering up the street.

"Sounds like it's over toward the hard road," I suggested. We walked over to Main Street which was the state highway.

When we got over there, Arnie said, "It's coming from the north. Maybe if we go up to the bridge we can see where it's at." So we went up through town, past the stores and filling stations and the sawmill. The bridge is where the highway and sidewalk cross high over the Illinois Central Railroad tracks. From up there, which is on the way to school, you can look right down into the smokestack of those huffing big old engines.

There weren't any trains to watch and the music was getting pretty loud. Some bigger kids were crossing the bridge, too, so we asked them what the music was. "Its a cal-ee-ope," one them said.

"What's that?" I asked.

"Aw, you know. One of them high steam cal-ee-opes. Like a big organ except its got more pipes and it steams or smokes."

Well now *that* we had to see, so we hurried up for two more blocks and sure enough there the thing was just like he said. It was huffin', and belchin', and clattering out "Over the Waves"—a mighty powerful sound.

Pretty soon the crowd was gathered up bigger than at prayer meeting, but quite a few of the same people. A fat man in a straw hat came out and told a couple of jokes. Then he picked up a banjo while another fellow got ready to play the accordion. Another guy had a whole set of drums—snare, cymbals, and bass, with a trap pedal he worked with his foot.

The fat man said, "Laydees and Gen-tul-mun. Here she is, Miss Zelda." And boy, there she was. She sort of slinked up to the edge of the stage which was just the back of a big flatbed truck. She just stood there wiggling, especially in the middle.

Just when I was trying to figure out how she was doing that, somebody put a hand on my shoulder. When I looked around, there was Mom. "You come with me," she said. I went. I didn't even say, "Aw Mom, do I have to?" There was just something about the way she looked that told me I'd better go quietly.

We had walked several blocks, and Mom hadn't said anything when I got to thinking about a few things. First, it was an awful long walk she took to find where I was, and then, somebody had to be staying with you kids. And how did she find out where I was?

Mom hadn't been feeling too good so I guess it was thinking about that walk that bothered me most. "I'm sorry you had to come and get me, Mom."

"It's all right, Junior. I shouldn't have had to," she said.

"What do you mean?"

"You shouldn't have gone without asking in the first place. You know that, don't you?"

She wasn't talking loud and mean. Just quiet and maybe a little sad like. It made me hurt inside when she talked like that. It was like there was something good between us and she was disappointed 'cause I'd ruined it.

"I shouldn't have to drag one of my children out of a medicine show that other people can go to, either," she went on. "I didn't see any other mothers from the church draggin' their kids out of there."

"I'm still sorry I didn't ask you and real sorry you had to take that long walk."

"It's all right, son. I know you won't do it again." Then she put an arm around my shoulders and patted me. At first that hurt me inside. Then I noticed she was actually leaning kind of heavy. For a while I walked very slow and straight to help hold her up.

At the hand bridge we stopped to rest. There Mom told me somebody had called the neighbors who had a phone and told on me. She had said I was at a place "not fit for the associational missionary's son." The neighbor lady stayed with you kids and Mom came after me.

We talked some more and I asked Mom if she was rested. She said, "Yes, but no rush. It's not often someone keeps the little ones and gives me a chance to get away for a few minutes these days."

Then she sort of giggled, like Mom doesn't do very often. "Maybe I wouldn't have to rest at all if I had a few swigs of that 'sweet elixir' that fat fellow was selling."

"Well, if it would make you move all over like Zelda, you'd get home in a hurry," I told her.

"Why Son, I didn't think you'd notice a thing like that." Then she did laugh, but my face was getting pretty red.

Anyway, when you get bigger, don't go to any medicine shows in your town. Better get out of the whole association. And if I can find a lady in the church whose tongue waggles like Zelda wiggles, then I'll know who told on me.

Memo 23: We Moved Again

It was quite a long time ago that I wrote the last memo to you. You have grown, we have moved two times, and you are getting ready to start the first grade. Any preacher's kid who is moving into a new town and starting to a new school needs help. I figure

I can give you some assistance since I've now lived in six towns and have attended eight schools.

There are a lot of nice people in Dowell. One thing we have learned in moving around is that there are many very nice people anywhere you go. Most of the time they will find you and make you feel welcome. If you ever think everybody is bad, you'd better take a look around again.

The members of the church sent a truck and four men to our old house in Dongola to help us move. They loaded and packed things so well that there was very little damage. When we got here we were tired and nervous, but they had a big surprise for us. Our dinner was all ready and waiting in the church basement, which is next door to the parsonage. All we had to do was sit down and eat. The ladies waited on us hand and foot, and the food was very good. You spent a lot of time looking and not much time eating, but you didn't spill anything. There was one lady there who will probably give us trouble before we move away. She reminds me of the first thing I want to tell you to be sure and remember. That is, watch out for the overly friendly people who make a big to-do welcoming you. They probably gave the last preacher and his family fits and are trying to make up for it.

The trouble is that they don't seem to like any preacher, so it won't be long until they will find something wrong with Dad. He will preach too loud or not be spiritual enough or not do enough visiting or will appoint a nominating committee instead of electing church officers in the annual meeting.

That lady who was gushing all over Mom wasn't doing any of the work. She wasn't dishing food or refilling iced tea glasses—nothing. The lady who was answering the other ladies' questions was over at the stove working and making the whole affair run smooth.

The bigmouthed lady has some kids she talked about. I'll tell you her name and point out the kids to you. Then you watch something. They will be very friendly and offer to help you get acquainted and do a lot of things. But when you need help they will be scarce. And in a few months they won't be friendly at all. That will be when their mother and father have started talking about Dad or his preaching.

You can help me watch for the deacon who will be Dad's best

friend. He will be the one Dad starts talking to the most when there is something wrong. He will be the man who helps prepare the new budget. He probably will be a tither and not get mad the first time Dad talks about giving. If he has kids they won't gush all over us. They will be polite and friendly and helpful for a long time. If his kids are bigger than any of us we will get their outgrown clothes, and they won't tell anyone they gave them to us.

At school you will be more on your own than at church. I won't see as many of your teachers and classmates as I see people at church so I can't give you as much firsthand information.

There are a few general things you can count on though. The teachers will try to help you and understand how you feel. They have to please the people in town, just like preachers do. Their children go through some of the same things preacher's children do.

There will be plenty of other kids at school who will be feeling just as bad as you do. They won't be talking to anyone else. Your best bet is to walk up to another kid who is by himself and say, "Hi, my name is P. H." If he gives you his name and smiles even a little bit, then you can explain to him that P. H. stands for Paul Henry. We just call you P. H. for short.

You don't have to tell him Uncle George calls you P. G. 'cause you aren't any bigger than a bar of soap.

Be careful of the kid who is the ringleader of the biggest gang. He's probably a bully and won't want anyone challenging him. If you haven't got any spunk and want to follow him like a lost sheep, then its OK to join his crowd. But I hope you have more backbone than that. If one of his gang tries to pick on you, don't start anything with that kid. The rest of them will gang up on you. Just go belt the daylights out of the bully. You'll be surprised at how many of his gang want to thump him and will help you out.

So far this sounds like you have to expect a lot of trouble, but that really isn't the case. There are many very nice people in Dowell. We have found friendly, helpful persons every place we have lived. There are just a few you have to look out for, especially the first few days in a new school or town. Don't let them worry you much. You are a likable little guy and a good little brother. You'll do just fine.

Dear Jr.

I can write sum now.
I can read most of what you write.
I have a friend Billy.
I like him.

> *Love,*
> *P. H.*

IV. Things, Food, and Games

A punster once referred to an acquaintance as "one of the world's greatest thingers." What he meant was that the person liked to build, study, and work with things. There was also a thinly veiled inference that the person was not a great thinker.

Mother used to despair of the things that Paul and I carried in our pockets. Dad preferred that we study rather than be "always fooling around with things." He also thought we wasted time playing games and eating.

Some psychological tests attempt to measure whether we associate with objects (things) or ideas (concepts). A triad of words is presented such as priest, temple, skyscraper. We are asked to choose the two words that are related. If temple and skyscraper are chosen, the association is of buildings—things. Choose temple and priest and you get a gold star. They denote a concept, religion. That's better than things according to some people.

It has been my experience that life is seldom composed of either/ or choices or situations. A lot of concepts can be learned by fooling around with things or by reacting with people while fooling around with things or playing games. And eating can have a great influence on the brain—like thinking about the next meal.

I'm not sure that there was always a concept associated with some of the things that meant much to me. But anyway, you may read what I wrote to Paul about some of those things, and you can be the judge.

Memo 24: Excess Cider

Dad preaches a sermon called "Don't do things in excess." He talks about doing all things in moderation. That means don't do too much of anything (work isn't included). Don't eat too much. Don't sleep too much. Don't sin at all; one sin is an excessive amount. Above all, don't drink too much.

That drinking rule is meant mostly for people who drink alcohol— beer, wine, whisky. Beer and whisky are so strong that one drink is too many, but a "little wine for the stomach's sake" may be permissible. The things you have to watch out for are the things Dad doesn't include in his sermon. Apple cider is one of those things.

I help make cider with lemon. I like to tell it that way because most people say, "I thought you made cider with apples." You really do, but I make cider with our neighbor, old Brother Lemon. He sells Lemon cider.

Every year I help him make gallons and gallons of cider for his regular customers. He makes plenty so he can store some in his cellar. I get at least a gallon to take home. If we make a lot, I get a gallon to sell for some extra money. It is easy to tell when cider time is getting close. Early in the year the old Fordson tractors moan and groan from morning until night. Some men told me that the gear box makes the noise and the big metal fenders act like sounding boards. The tractor is used to pull the spraying machine which is a wooden tank with a gas engine and a punp on it.

When the spraying is all done you don't hear the old tractor in the orchard until they start picking the apples and pulling wagons loaded with them. About then Brother Lemon stops by to ask, "Are you going to be busy in a day or two?" He knows I'm waiting for him and won't be too busy to help him, but he always asks.

When we go to the orchard I take my wagon and he pushes a wheelbarrow. We take empty gallon jugs, some galvanized buckets, and two or three empty baskets. The first place we stop is the sorting shed. Mr. Lemon goes up to the end of the grading machine where apples are being unloaded from the orchard. He studies the apples for a long time like he's seeing what kind looks the best. Then he comes back along the big belts with holes in them that the different sized apples fall through. Somewhere along there he finds just what he is looking for. It's usually two, sometimes three, different kinds of apples, medium size, and fully ripened. He sets his selection to one side then we load them and take them to the cider mill and press at the edge of the orchard.

My work starts in earnest then. There is water to haul to wash the apples, the mill, and the press. The baskets of apples have to be set out of the wagon and wheelbarrow and sometimes we go back for more apples. Finally, I turn the crank as we grind the apples Mr. Lemon feeds into the mill. Sometimes he cranks when I get tired.

As we are grinding, some juice begins to run out of the apples as they fall into the press. A funnel catches it and runs it into a jug. When the press is full we turn the top down on it with a big screw and wheel. The sides of the press are wooden slats that have cracks in between them. As the top is screwed down, the ground up apples get squeezed; the juice runs out between the slats and down into the trough below. At the end of the trough Brother Lemon sets the funnel and jug.

You have to squeeze a lot of apples to fill a jug. All that hauling and washing and cranking makes a fellow pretty thirsty. That's why Brother Lemon brings along a tin cup. He samples the cider to see that it tastes OK. He gives me the cup and I give it a taste. He can tell the difference between *good* and *pretty good* cider, but I can't. When you're thirsty, it all tastes very good. I kept sampling the cider and in between samples take a big drink to keep from getting too thirsty.

After a few drinks Brother Lemon says, "Be careful. Don't overdo it, Son." I pay attention to him now, but the first time I helped him I didn't listen soon enough.

That first time the cider was not too warm and was very sweet. It was what I call "real good." I kept sampling, but each sample just made me thirstier. Pretty soon my tummy felt warm. Not a bad feeling, just warm like maybe another drink would cool it. Then the warm feeling went over to the left side, then over to the right side—sort of rolled around down inside there. Finally it sort of settled low over on the left and began to change from warm to kind of crampy.

Then all of a sudden I knew why Brother Lemon had said to be careful. But you know, there wasn't a toilet in sight. And I knew I didn't have time to go looking for one.

"You're just going to have to stay here in the orchard, Son. Just pick out any tree and hide behind it best you can. It'll be good for next year's crop."

I found a big tree not far away. Luckily, the mowing machine can't cut too close to the trees so there were a few weeds between me and the sorting shed. By the time Brother Lemon brought me some newspaper, I was feeling better. He was very kind. He didn't laugh—at least not where I could see him.

Now when Dad preaches about excess I think of cider. It sure proves that a little bit of some things can be too much. Another thing I'll tell you about sometime is leaving the cork just a little bit loose on the cider jug. Just a little bit loose for a couple of weeks is another kind of excess, and you have to keep that jug hidden from Dad.

Memo 25: Batteries from Theater Alley

Kids in our family don't get to go to the theater. Dad says they show "filthy pictures." In fact, Dad never says shows or theater without saying *filthy* first.

When I say something about other kids seeing a show made about a good book I have read, he quotes part of the Bible to me. Usually its something like, "If eating meat causes my brother to be offended, I will eat no meat." I hope I never meet any people who get offended over hamburgers or hot dogs. I already know a lot of them who don't like movies.

All of that to-do about shows doesn't make it wrong to look at the outside of the theater. Out front there is a big electric sign called a marquee. The lights on it seem to chase each other around, but they really don't. What happens is that they take turns going out and coming back on. Someday I'm going to find out how they do that.

It is interesting to poke around in the alley behind the show house. The spilled popcorn gets swept out there. The kernels that didn't pop get thrown out the backdoor. Birds, mostly sparrows, have a feast. Mice do too, and sometimes we see a rat come out from under a coal shed and eat corn.

If you ever get behind the theater, you may as well wander on down the alley. While the theater smells of old butter and popcorn, the book store smells like ink on a fresh newspaper, the variety store smells dirty, and the clothing store stinks like mothballs. It's hard to smell the clothing store when the weather is warm since it is just across from the blacksmith shop. I can't tell you what it smells like, but you will learn that putting shoes on horses makes some of them awful nervous.

We find a lot of good junk and some other interesting things under and in back of the book store. A professional boxer trains under there. He has a punching bag which he can make dance up against an upside down platform fastened to the ceiling. He also has a 38 automatic pistol he keeps in his clothes bag. I saw it one day and the barrel was pointing right up out of the bag at me. The hole in the barrel looks very big when you see it that way.

The old books that get thrown out aren't usually very good. They are too old or too torn up.

The best junk is the dead batteries. Some of them have just enough juice left in them to make static on my headphones. If Blair and I make up we'll make a phone again with our headphones and the batteries will make it work better. We stick one wire of the phones into the ground and just use one long wire to hook up the other wires. If we stick an old battery in there and talk through it, it helps but not long 'cause those old batteries aren't much good.

There was an ad in the paper saying they bought old batteries over at the junk place where we sell old iron. We hauled the batteries from behind the book store over there one day. It was a hard job and then the man said he meant old car batteries; he wanted to get the lead out of them. He wouldn't even let us dump the batteries we had on his lot. We had to haul them and hide them someplace else. We sure didn't want to take them all the way back to the book store.

I saved a couple of the batteries and tore them apart. The connector clips on the top of them are real neat. I'm saving them for making phones and crystal sets. In the middle of the number 2 dry cells is the biggest stick of carbon. Its long and black and round. You can write on the sidewalk with it. I figured I could use a chunk of it for a crystal in my radio but it didn't work. When I read the book again it said some crystals are Carborundum, not carbon. There's a big difference between them. I scratched that cat whisker all over that chunk of carbon and didn't find a single hot spot.

Mostly old dry batteries just make a mess when they are torn up. They have a lot of sticky, pasty stuff inside. When I lay them on the back porch and bash them with a hammer, Mom thinks it makes too much noise and might wake up you little ones. Sometimes you don't sleep good.

The sticky stuff also gets on the porch. Mom made me scrub it off and that wasn't easy. She said, "What did you bring those dirty things home for?"

"Well, they didn't cost anything and I thought I could get some money for them or get some good parts off of them."

"Did you?" she wanted to know.

"Nope."

"Well, that's generally the way it is, Son. When you get something for nothing that usually is just what it is worth."

Memo 26: Shinny Sticks

There is very little money for toys at our house. We have a few things that were bought new and some more that were given to us secondhand. We have fun with scooters made with boards and skates and old wagon wheels. The round bottoms out of bean hampers can be rolled just like a hoop. The heavy wooden drive wheel from an old thrasher knocks over milk cans just like bowling. Girls mostly play hopscotch and boys play shinny.

Its great fun to play shinny. There is a brick road that crosses our street on top of the hill and half-a-block from our house. The alley marks the middle of the block so we use it for center and play on the whole block.

One boy can play shinny by himself, but it is a lot more fun if there is a whole gang. All you need is a tin can—a small milk can is best—and a shinny stick. One boy can pretend he is playing golf or shinny when he is alone, but that keeps you from starting the game at center where all the fun starts.

The game begins when the can is placed on center. Two players face each other with the can between them. They hold their shinny sticks on the ground on the side of the can that is opposite the goal they are going toward. On the count of *one* the sticks are raised and touched together above the can. Then the sticks go back to the ground. At the count of *two* the sticks are raised and touched, and put down again. Then on *three* up the sticks come, touch, and the game is on when the fastest center man hits the can to knock it toward the goal.

Some funny things can happen on *three.* Shinny sticks have straight handles, but on the bottom end they are turned up where they are supposed to hit the can. They look something like an upside down walking stick. Sometimes on *three* one center will try to hook the other center's stick. Then he'll try to unhook fast and hit the can. Sometimes both fellows hit the can at the same time. Then the can is either caught dead still between the sticks or flies out just any way. It may hit shins, eyes, hands—just any old place, and it hurts.

Once the can is knocked from center, everybody tries to hit it and knock it toward and over the goal. With a whole gang on each side the game sure is lively and rough. The can keeps hitting people. Players miss the can and hit someone. Somebody trips or slips and falls. Back and forth and back and forth the game goes. When we play the whole block, it takes a long time to score. Finally, the can gets knocked over the goal line then we all sit down and rest.

When a car comes down the street we have to quit playing until it passes. People in cars don't like to go down the shinny street because sometimes the can hits their cars or some kid hits the cars with his stick. If we stop for a car then two kids closest to the can face off and start again just like at center after the car has passed. We argue about where the can was before the car came by.

The people along the street don't care for our game except maybe those who have kids who play. Player's parents don't say much but sometimes the other grown-ups stick their head out the door and holler, "My land, you kids sure do make a racket."

It's almost as much fun hunting shinny sticks as it is playing shinny. Early in the spring we go to Cratsinger Hollow and bring back two or three sticks for each one of us. A good shinny stick needs to cure, dry out, and you have to have a spare or two in case your favorite stick gets broken or stolen.

We hunt sticks in Cratsinger 'cause there is a cave out there. It has a small entrance that makes you crawl in the water to get in. Then there is a big room that is dark and wet and has a ledge in it up over the entrance. When we climb up on the ledge we can look out a hole that is like a round window and see the sissies who are out there and afraid to come into the cave.

Shinny sticks are best if they come from hickory or oak trees. We call them ironwood trees because they are so tough. Good sticks grow on the north side of very steep hills. That's because trees on the north don't get as much sunshine as the other sides so they grow slower. The hills also make the tree grow out sideways from its roots then turn up toward what light there is. That's what puts the crook on the end of the stick.

If you get tired hunting you can settle for just any old stick, but it's worth looking for just the right conditions to get the best stick. It's like that with a lot of things. Look for or wait for the best situation and then you can get what is really worthwhile.

Memo 27: BB Guns

BB guns can't be trusted. They have gotten me in trouble twice. The first time wasn't so bad because I was just in the first grade. The last time was just a couple of days ago, and I almost got beat up over it.

When we lived in Cobden and I had just started to school, I used to help Ron shoot his BB gun. He did most of the shooting while I did the other things—like carrying the BBs, picking up the birds he shot, or finding tin cans or bottles to shoot when there weren't many birds.

Usually we didn't get into trouble. Oh, we got me into trouble with Dad once when I put some dead blackbirds under a kettle. There were three of them and they were so pretty and purple I thought I'd save them for a few days to look at them. So I turned the kettle upside down over them to protect them.

The weather was warm. I forgot the birds until Dad smelled an awful smell and asked what was under the kettle. When I told him, he said for me to get the shovel and bury them. I got the shovel but when the kettle was lifted, the birds looked and smelled horrible. They made me sick at my stomach. Dad had to bury them. They made him gag a lot, but he did it.

The first real bad trouble came when Ron's dad was picking bunch beans from his garden. Most pole beans can be picked while a person is standing up. Bunch beans are different. They grow on the short plants so you have to hunker down or bend over to pick them. Ron's dad wasn't hunkered, he was bending over with his head in the opposite direction from us.

Ron was aiming the gun. He'd been aiming it all around like he was just trying out the sight—not shooting a thing. Two or three times he aimed it sort of at the garden, like he was sighting on a tomato stake or a red pepper.

Finally he said, "You can pull the trigger if you want to." Well, I'd been hunting cans and bottles and not shooting at all. I was just dying to shoot that gun once, so I pulled the trigger. Then things got trampled in the bean patch.

Ron's dad gave a powerful grunt and stood up very straight with his right hand over his back pocket. Then he turned around and came running at Ron and me. He wasn't a careful runner. He forgot to run down the rows of bean plants. He just came a sashawayin' catywampus through the beans with his face getting redder by the minute. It looked like his face was puffing up, and about the time he got even with me I thought he would burst. Before he got there Ron handed me the gun and said, "Here, you'd better take this." Then he ran around behind the house.

His Dad ran right by me and was catching up with Ron real fast the last I saw of them. As he went by he grabbed the gun right out of my hands. "Here, give me that."

I decided it was time I was getting on home, so I left.

At supper that night Dad asked, "How come you boys shot Mr. Norris with that BB gun?"

You know, I kinda thought that was what happened, but I wasn't ready to admit anything yet.

"We did?"

"Come on now. You were right there and saw what happened."

"I was right there and saw it happen, but I wasn't holding any BB gun." I told him truthfully.

"Did you touch the gun?" Dad wasn't going to quit until he had the story straight.

"Just with one finger."

"That's all it takes on the trigger."

Dad seemed to be having a little trouble keeping from grinning. That made me feel a little better.

"I guess you're right," I told him.

"Mr. Norris told me what happened, Son. He knows you didn't aim that gun at him."

Then he kind of ruffled up my hair and told me, "Bigger boys sometimes try to blame littler ones to keep out of trouble. You have to learn to watch out for that."

I've found out Dad sure knew what he was talking about. For a preacher he knows a lot about things preachers don't look like they ever would know about.

I thought about Ron and his gun today when Judy almost beat me up just because Blair's BB gun doesn't shoot straight.

Judy is a lot bigger than I am, and he gets pretty rough when we play. I tell him he has a girl's name. He punches me around a lot and calls me "Shrimp." I do things to get even with him like putting crawdads in his pocket. Today I don't think I was trying to get even with him for anything. It was just one of those things. You just can't trust some guns.

Judy was working on his bicycle. He had it turned upside down, resting on the seat and handle bars, while he leaned over working on the chain.

Blair was letting me shoot cans. I'd bought some BBs and he was trading me some shots for part of the BBs. When I saw old Judy bent over that way, I thought I'd give him a little scare.

When Blair saw where I was aiming he said, "You'd better not do that."

"How do you know what I'm aiming at?" I asked him.

"You're aiming at Judy."

"No, I'm not. I'm sighting right past his hind end at that oil can on the step. Take a look."

Blair got behind me and sighted down the barrel. "Better not try it. It's too close."

"I can do it. I'm a good shot." So I took careful aim alongside of Judy and at the can and pulled the trigger.

I know I'm a good shot and I aimed real good. At best I only meant to snib Judy by his hip if I missed the can a little to the left. But either that gun didn't shoot true or Judy swayed a little toward the BB. I was pretty sure I saw him flinch.

He didn't move though. Even his hand holding the wrench didn't move, and it was moving before I shot. That holding real still like that was what tipped me off that I'd better start moving. That old Judy had been hit. I didn't hear no BB hit the oil can. He was just holding still until I figured I'd missed everything and took my eye off of him. Then he was going to do something I wouldn't like.

I was closer to my back door than Judy was, so I dropped the gun in front of Blair and took off in a dead run. Judy started a split second later.

I can usually outrun Judy in a race, even if he does have longer legs. This time, though, he was moving faster than usual. That BB must have wound him up. I could tell by the way he was moving I didn't have time to go around by the culvert so I headed in a straight line over the ditch and for the backdoor. Usually on my best jump I can't get clean across that ditch, but I made it that time. I also jumped over the back fence about two steps ahead of Judy.

He had a problem then. We both had to go past the side of the garage. I was going straight past it, and Judy was angling in from the left so he had to make a turn when he came down from jumping the fence. He skidded on that turn, landed in the tomatoes, and I hit the back porch and went through the door. Mom was in the kitchen and she said, "What's your rush?"

"I'm going to the bathroom." And I did. I locked the door too.

I heard old Judy light on the porch and start pawing the screen door. He must have seen Mom 'cause he didn't come in.

"What do you want?" Mom asked him.

"I want that ____ kid of yours," Judy yelled. "He shot me."

"You best mind your tongue, young man. I won't stand for that kind of language around this house."

"I'm gonna beat that kid of yours to a pulp if I can get my hands on him," Judy howled.

"You'll do no such thing," Mom warned him. "You're much bigger than he is, and I'll have his father call the police if you so much as touch him."

I was feeling better, but it was a good thing I was in the bathroom 'cause about then I really had to go. Must have been all that hard running.

"But he shot me," Judy insisted.

"You look pretty healthy to me to be shot." Mom informed him. "What is that green stain on your overalls? It looks like tomato stain. Smells like it too. Have you been in our garden?"

"Aw, go to ____." And Judy stomped off the porch.

"You mind your tongue, young man, or I'll tell your father."

I heard Mom walk up to the other side of the bathroom door. "You can come out now, fraidy cat. Judy's gone. And you'd better let BB guns alone after this. And you'd better tie up those tomatoes before your father gets back."

I'd fix those tomatoes, all right, as soon as Judy went back to his own neighborhood. But I wasn't going out in that backyard until I was sure there was no Judy, no Blair, and no BB guns anyplace out there.

Memo 28: First or Last

Preacher's kids are almost always at the front of the line or the back of the line. They are seldom in the middle. You can expect to have the lead part in school and church plays, or you will probably not even be in the cast. Then maybe you can sell tickets or help build the scenery.

It's kind of like that with parties too. Either people want you because they are in the church and want the preacher's kid to make it look like a church social, or they don't want you around in case they want to dance or play card games. You are going to get pretty old before you go to a party where they play post office. I'll tell you about that game someday.

What I like best is the way being first or last—in this case, first— helps me with the baseball team. Kids bigger than me can't even make the team, but I did and I get to bat first. In fact, they just keep me on the team for the batting part. They don't let me do too much fielding.

I get to bat first because I'm sort of short. When I just sort of hunker down the umpire calls most of the pitches *balls*. That way I get to walk most of the time. Those bigger guys always say, "Don't swing at a thing. Just stand in there and keep your head down."

I get to first base nearly every game. Even if I don't walk, I get to bunt. Playing with bigger kids teaches you to run fast, so I can beat out most bunts and get on first that way.

Then the fun really starts. Those big guys on our team can hit or they bunt also, and I'm supposed to scoot over to the next base.

It's fun to get to score the first run of the game.

Fielding is something else, though. So far they don't trust me. Most of the time I play right field 'cause most of the other team's batters are right-handed and hit the ball to left field.

Our guys really rub it in about my fielding when a left-handed batter comes up. They yell, "Time out. Hey, Shorty, get over into left field for this batter." Then the whole game stops while me and the left fielder swap places.

If one of the bigger guys drops a fly ball, I used to really yell at him. But then I found out if I yelled and we were a run or two ahead they'd take me out of the game and make me sit on the bench. So usually I just keep quiet, swap fields, and hope to stay in the game.

When we play on the diamond across from the junior high I sometimes get to play center field. My fly ball catching isn't too bad. My experience with clotheslines is a lot better than Jake's. He's the regular center fielder.

Jake is a very fast runner. He is also a very good fly ball catcher. His biggest problem is that he doesn't always look where he is going. He steps in holes in the outfield. When we play in Crowe's pasture he steps in other things, and he runs into other fielders a lot. I know I'm much smaller than he is, and I'm not supposed to be such a hot fielder, so I stay out of his way.

One day we were playing across from the school, and Jake was feeling pretty good that day. He'd caught a few long flies and was beginning to yell at other players and rob the other fielder and me of catches.

Then somebody hit a high hard one deep into center over Jake's head. He started running back very fast while looking over his shoulder. He forgot all about the clothesline until some time after he hit it. It caught him up alongside his neck. The wire sagged but it didn't break. Jake seemed to hang by his neck for a moment while his feet went up into the air. Then his whole body sort of leveled out and down he came. He landed on his back and just lay there. He had a silly grin on his face. A big red welt came up on his neck. He was breathing OK, and pretty soon he opened his eyes, got up, and staggered to the bench.

"Put Smitty in center for a while," he gasped. So I got to play center field. None of the bigger guys tried to talk the captain out of it.

So now I'm the center fielder when we play that diamond 'cause I'm not as high as the clothesline.

Dad reads the Scripture that says something about the last being first and the first being last. I don't think it meant baseball, especially, but its kind of appropriate.

I don't mind being first or last most of the time. It's trying to figure out which one you're supposed to be at the moment that is the great big problem.

Memo 29: Fish or Fat Pork?

"Thou shalt not bear false witness [lie]."

That Commandment is going to cause you a lot of trouble. Part of the trouble will come because of the lies you tell. Much of the problem will result from lies other people tell you.

Kids go through a lot of what Mom calls *phases*. It seems to me there are three phases of kid's lies. The first one is when you just get to wanting or thinking something so hard you really get to believing it when it isn't so.

Take wanting to swim, for instance. You think about it a lot and it sure would be fun to swim. After awhile you are sure you could swim if you had a chance. Pretty soon you have been thinking about it so long it seems you just get to feeling you've been swimming, so you tell somebody you can. About then is when you finally get a chance to go to the creek, and you get caught in a lie. You can't really swim. At best you can only dog paddle with one toe touching bottom. The guys won't let you get by with that.

Then there are lies that shock people. You just make up a yarn that's such a whopper no one in their right mind would believe it. You can tell a girl you saw a ghost. She knows there aren't any ghosts, but she still will take a deep breath and ask, "Where did you see him?" Girls always think ghosts are hims.

The worst phase of lie telling is when you get caught doing something, and you have to try to lie to get out of it. If you steal something, you say somebody gave it to you. If you go to a show, you say you went to somebody's house. And if you eat your sister's candy, you just say you didn't do it.

After you've got caught lying a few times, you find it's best to own up to what you got caught doing in the first place. That way you only get a licking for one thing instead of two.

One reason kids get confused is that grown-ups are pretty good at lying. And they are so slick that it's hard to catch them at it. They don't often come right out and tell a barefaced lie. Usually they do one of two things. They tell you half of the truth or they ask you a question that tricks you into believing the wrong thing.

I get that half-truth thing pulled on me when I have to stay and look after you little kids while Mom and Dad go someplace. Mom will say, "Junior, I want you to take care of the kids for a while. Daddy and I are going with the Millers."

The Millers have a car and they take the folks visiting and other places. Naturally I want to know how long I'm going to be stuck at home so I ask, "Where are you going?"

"Oh, we're going up through town."

Now that's true as far as it goes. It's supposed to sound like "We're going up to town," in case I'm not listening good. But they aren't just going to town. They're going through town and out by Big Creek visiting or to a wedding and I'm going to keep you kids for a long time. Mom doesn't dress up and put on the cologne the ladies class gave her for Christmas just to buy groceries.

The question asking trick is the thing Mom just pulled on me that caused me to write this to you.

Maybe I'd better go back a little bit and tell you about fat pork. We call it "fat pork" because that sounds better than "pork bellies." You don't care much for it, but you eat a little bit of it. It's better than going hungry.

When we get the relief order we order fat pork or salt pork because we are expected to and because Mom can do a lot with it. That pork comes in kind of a flat round chunk bigger than my two hands spread out, and its about a couple of inches thick. It looks mostly white and is covered with salt.

Mom puts chunks of it in beans and boils them together. That's not bad, especially if we have some corn bread to go with it. Other times she slices it like bacon and fries it. If the salt pork has some pink threads of lean in it, it's almost as good as bacon with eggs. But you have to be careful not to salt the eggs when they have been fried in the pork grease.

Some of that pork hasn't got any lean in it at all. Mom just heats it in the oven to get the grease out of it. Some of the grease is poured into a mason jar for cooking lard. The poorest grease goes into a crock to be mixed with lye to make soap. The soap is pretty strong, so we mostly use it for clothes or when somebody gets chiggers or poison ivy.

Sometimes Mom puts some other stuff and perfume in good grease and makes pretty soap.

The best part of heating pork for grease is getting the cracklins. That's the part of the rind—outside or skin—that's left brown and chewy after the fat has been melted off. You like cracklins and get along with them pretty good. Oh, once in a while after you have chewed one until it's limber and slick, it tries to go down the wrong way. If you can't cough it up, usually Mom or Dad or me stick our finger down your throat and crook our finger around the cracklin and haul it out. You get kind of red-faced and watery-eyed, but you aren't choked too bad yet.

But to finish what I started to tell you. We sat down to dinner today and there wasn't too much to eat except beets and turnip greens and some meat fried in cornmeal. It was sliced in thin pieces and the cornmeal was pretty thick. At first I wasn't too sure what it was so I asked Mom, "What kind of meat is this?"

She said, "What does it look like?"

I'd been thinking about that some, so I took another look where I'd bitten off a piece. "Well, it sort of looks like catfish, but. . . ."

Mom interrupted me right there. "It does look like catfish, doesn't it?"

You know, she made it sound like it was fish sure enough. The only question seemed to be what kind of fish was it.

I didn't completely figure out what Mom was pulling on me right that very minute. However, the longer I chewed on that piece of fat pork the surer I was that it wasn't catfish. Besides, we have cabbage in the garden and if that had been honest to goodness fish we'd have had cole slaw with it.

So there you have it about lying. You'll lie some. I hope not too much so that you get in trouble. You can take some comfort by thinking that most kids lie some time, and even mommas don't tell the whole truth when all the meat they have to cook is salt pork.

Dear Jr.

I rode your bike today.
It rides pretty good.
I do not ride very good.
Your bike has a broke pedal.
Dad is not mad. He says you will be mad.

> *Love,*
> *P. H.*

V.   Child Theology

Are you aware that you may represent God to some people, especially children? That is a sobering thought, isn't it?

I developed my concept of God by observing and listening to older people. There were many persons, located in many towns and churches, who were more real to me than the things I read about God.

Learning about God by observing is according to his plan. He has revealed himself to man through his Son. He sent Jesus to be seen in person by many people. We learn about God by studying the records of men with whom he lived and worked; men whom he taught with words and deeds.

I'm sure that much of what was learned from Dad, other ministers, dozens of deacons, and a host of church members, was not formal theology. But my theology was developed to a large degree by watching and listening to all of those people. Then by doing many of the things they taught me, I learned about God by relating to him and experiencing him.

I'm grateful to those who loved me enough to help me understand; to those teachers who taught me in school and Sunday School; and to those who were setting a good example many times when they were not aware that a little kid was watching.

To P. H., who was a loving little listener, I left the following (theological?) memos. Perhaps they did a better job of giving him a correct theology than my actions did.

Memo 30: The Broken-plate Sermon

Old Brother Barker is an evangelist. You are going to see a lot of preachers who are called evangelists. They come around for a couple of weeks about every six months. They stir everybody up and then go back where they came from or go to another meeting.

Most of them get paid a freewill offering which sometimes means you keep passing the plate until you get at least the smallest amount he is expecting. Evangelists get more per week than Dad does, but he says they don't get paid every week like he's supposed to.

I've heard some evangelists talking to Dad about the offerings being kind of small. They want him to urge everyone to put more in the plate. It doesn't seem right for Dad to have to ask for more money for someone else when he doesn't always get his salary when it's supposed to be payday.

Some evangelists try to be funny about money. They say, "It always makes me nervous when Brother Smith talks about money. But then it makes me sick when he doesn't, and I'd rather be nervous than sick." Most of the congregation laughs and I guess some of them pay a little more. Over a few meetings that joke might be worth quite a few dollars. By now I wouldn't give you too much for it.

Brother Barker stirred up quite a fuss over some china plates. Offerings weren't very good to begin with and I think they fell off some more after the sermon he preached with the plates.

Dad tried to talk him out of preaching that sermon, but he didn't do any good at it. Then he suggested using old plates, but he didn't win that argument-discussion either.

You see, the idea was to preach a sermon about the Ten Commandments. For each Commandment a big number was painted on a plate. Brother Barker would talk about the Commandment for a while. Then he'd holler loud that most of the congregation had broken that Commandment to smithereens. As he yelled that he'd smack one of those new plates with a hammer and break it just the way the Commandment had been broken.

It all looked exciting, especially from the front row where I had to sit to keep out of trouble until the mourners started showing up during the invitation. There was this stack of brand new plates on one side of the pulpit and a cardboard box on the other side.

You could tell when Brother Barker was about to run out of things to say about a Commandment. He'd lay his Bible on top of his notes and start fumbling for a plate with his left hand. Then he'd fish the hammer out of the box. Right when he said, "and you've broken," he'd smack that plate dead center and break it. Most of the pieces went into the box, but a lot of little chips flew onto the choir and out onto my seat.

To my way of thinking that was a risky sermon for a man to preach. I kept wondering what would happen if he hit his thumb with the hammer. He might hurt it bad enough that he'd break that Commandment about taking the Lord's name in vain. He could cut his finger and bust that one too.

All during the sermon he wasn't making friends with the women in the choir. They hated to see good plates being ruined like that. To make it worse, they hated to have to brush little pieces of plate off of them, especially pieces of brand new plates. I've eaten off of many of those ladies' tables and they don't have good plates, not brand new ones, not matched sets of old plates, either. They thought it was a sinful waste to break up good plates.

After that night, some people complained to the deacons and to Dad. He and Brother Barker talked about what to do for a long time. The next night Dad announced that the dishes were a very cheap set from the Riteway store which was owned by one of the deacons.

The following night he had to explain that the Riteway didn't just sell cheap dishes. They had good merchandise, but the dishes that were broken were the least expensive. That didn't stop all the fuss.

Finally, the deacon decided to donate the dishes. This was announced, and it stopped a few tongues from wagging. I still heard a few remarks about "scandalous waste."

Now I can't prove anything, but if you and me could bet, I'd bet you that those plates weren't donated. Oh, the bill was probably marked paid and given to the church treasurer. What I think happened is that the deacon held back the price of the plates from his freewill offering. I tried to see if he slipped anything into the plate when he took up the collection, but I really couldn't tell.

There weren't enough invitations for Brother Barker to eat out the last of the week. Mom had to feed him at our house, on a plate that didn't match a thing on the table.

Memo 31: The Sweet-potato Revival

I don't want you to get the idea that Brother Barker's revival was all bad. There were some good things about it. Lots of food was probably the best part.

It's funny how arrangements for the evangelist vary. Sometimes he gets a room and breakfast somewhere. If he stays at a boarding-house, he gets breakfast. If the man of the house goes to work late or is retired he gets breakfast. Otherwise he gets up early and comes over to our house for breakfast. That's supposed to keep down some kind of talk.

I like it better when he comes to our house. The members give Mom lots of eggs and bacon, and some actually give her some ham. It doesn't matter whether its the shank end of the ham from a regular member or the butt end from the deacon who owns the Riteway, ham is good with eggs.

I always get one egg and a little piece of the meat. Mom sees to that. And depending on whether Brother Barker eats two eggs or three, I might get another one. I'd hate to see a preacher get sick right in the middle of revival, but I can't see it would hurt if he just got off his feed a little at breakfast time.

Another thing that is good is when we all get invited out. I just love to hear one of the ladies say, "Sister Smith, why don't you and the children come along with the preachers?" That way we get to ride in a car sometimes. Oh, we have to get all cleaned up in the middle of the day, but a good meal is worth getting your face washed and your hair combed an extra time. It's really worth the bother if you go out to a country member's house.

The real problem starts if the visiting preacher brags on something too early in the first week. That's what Brother Barker did. He and Dad went out for the evening meal the very first Monday. Now I'm not saying who the lady was 'cause she's my Sunday School teacher, but she fixed sweet potates. But she mashed up those potatoes and baked them with marshmallows on top of them.

Brother Barker must have eaten a big bait of those potatoes. He came to church rubbing his stomach and taking on about how good they were. He got right up in the pulpit and while he was saying the good things to get on the right side of the crowd, he got to bragging up the potatoes some more. If he'd known a sweet potato joke, you can bet he would have told it.

It wasn't hard to figure out what was going to happen after that. He and Dad were going to have to eat a lot of sweet potatoes. Most of the women put the marshmallows on top, but some added honey or sorghum to the potatoes. Others fixed sweet potato pie. For a few days it wasn't too bad, but then those two preachers got burnt out on sweet potatoes and couldn't stuff down another bite of them. That's when they started bringing dishes and pans of sweet potatoes home to Mom.

All those ladies who were fixing potatoes for the evangelist had stuffed too many of them into their own family a long time ago. Every year at harvest time they overdid it. So they weren't about to keep all those leftovers. We got them, and for a while it was fine.

Then we began to hate the sight of sweet potatoes. Mom kept setting them back. Some of them she canned. Some of them she gave to neighbors who weren't members of our church. Our whole end of town got pretty full of sweet potatoes.

It's funny the way different people remember different revivals or evangelists. Some people remember Brother Barker because of the plates. We remember him at our house because of the plates and the potatoes.

Some people remember a revival by who got saved—like when an aunt or an uncle or a cousin got saved. Or they think of the time the town drunk got religion.

At our house we remember the creamed-asparagus revival, the green-bean meeting, or the strawberry-preserve evangelist. If you don't separate them that way, all those different revivals sort of run together in your mind after a while.

I've got a suggestion for some of those visiting preachers. They ought to eat their first meal at our house. That way Mom can fix something we haven't had for a long time or can't afford very often. That way their bragging can get us something we have been a little short on.

About the time they get burnt out on something, they could come back to our house so Mom could switch dishes. I think it would be fun to have a pork-loin-roast revival, but a fried-liver revival sure wouldn't appeal to very many preacher's kids.

Memo 32: Let Jesus Do It

Some day you are going to start feeling bad and you won't know why. It will be different than when you feel bad from eating too much catsup and peas with fresh strawberries. When it's from something you ate, you feel bad in your stomach. You can locate that and tell where the bad feeling is. What I want to tell you about is a horrible feeling you can't locate. It's even different than when you get the wind knocked out of you.

The first time I noticed the feeling was when I was about eight years old. There was just the puny feeling all over that I couldn't get rid of. Nothing caused it so far as I could tell. It hung on for a few days then I didn't notice it for quite a spell.

Another time when the feeling came back there still was no reason for it. I can remember that time I felt like I do when I've done something very bad and been bawled out something awful. When that happens you go around acting smart like you don't care and are having fun. All the while you don't really feel good inside yourself.

The storms we had that summer sure didn't make me feel any better. Where we lived there were a lot of windstorms with plenty of rain and thunder and lightning. They usually came in the afternoon or evening after several hours of hot, sultry weather.

There would be a few clouds showing up over the low hills to the south and west. Those clouds would move closer and get higher. Some of them would build way up high and you could actually see them rolling at the top and going up and up. Dad called them thunderheads.

About the time one of the thunderheads got high enough to blot out the sun, there would be a batch of dark clouds piling up below the high ones. The low clouds laid out horizontal and had light and dark streaks that sort of rolled over and over as they came closer. The real bad storms turned yellow or greenish as they came on.

Before the storm got to us, there would often be a long, quiet spell. Then the wind would blow cool. That felt good, but you knew there was trouble coming. Then a few great big drops of rain would splatter like bombs in the dust. If we weren't home then, that was the last chance to run for the house or get wet.

As the storm came close the lightning would start and get brighter. The time in between lightning flashes and thunders would get shorter and shorter.

Finally there would be a flash and a crash all at the same time. Fire would roll along the ground or streak up a tree. Then the rain would come down in sheets.

During one of those storms I thought our house would blow away. Our backdoor was on the west side of the house. The rain blew right straight in under the back-porch roof. First the door blew open. The table oilcloth and newspapers scattered all over the house, and the reading lamp tipped over. Dad and I managed to push the door shut but not before a lot of water blew in. Water kept coming under and around the door. Dad and I got wet and Mom took to mopping the floor and wringing the water from the mop into a bucket. She'd empty the bucket out the front door and mop some more.

Dad made you and the other kids get under the beds. The girls got to crying and your eyes got very big, but you didn't cry.

About the time my arms got so tired I didn't think I could hold the door any more, the wind began to die down. Then it whipped around from the other direction, but that didn't last long.

When it was all over there was lots of water in the ditches. There were limbs in yards and on the road. I found a lot of torn up bird nests. The sky over east where the storm went stayed dark for a long time. The lightning kept flashing in the distance. The thunder got down to a rumble, then we couldn't hear it any more.

After the storm I felt very bad in addition to being scared inside.

About a week or so after the storm, a revival started at our church. Preacher Wilson came to be the evangelist. He really wasn't a scary preacher, but I kept feeling bad listening to him.

It seemed like the longer he preached the worse I felt. I liked him all right, but something about the way he kept waving his arms and yelling and threatening hell fire upset me.

Then there was that little window up in the point of the wall behind him. I didn't like to look right at Brother Wilson so I looked past him at that little window.

But one night that got pretty scary too. I was looking at the window and saw a little flicker of light. *Heat lightning,* I thought.

Then it flickered again. *That's toward the east,* I said to myself.

Can't be storm lightning. It's heat lightning. And it kept getting brighter and with longer flashes. Old Brother Wilson was getting louder. The flashes got brighter. I got more scared.

He kept slapping his Bible on the pulpit and that reminded me of thunder. When he was beginning to wind up for the finish, he yelled, "And if I wasn't prepared to die, I'd be scared to death."

Oh boy, right then I knew what was making me feel so puny. I was just plain scared. Scared of dying, but it really hadn't come clear to me why I was scared.

Then I began to remember a lot of the things in Dad's sermons, in the daily Bible readings, and what some of my Sunday School teachers had been saying. I was what they called *under conviction.* What I needed was to be saved. I didn't do anything about it right then. A lot of people were going up front, and it seemed likely a fellow could get lost up there.

For a few nights I kept getting more scared and wondering if I'd live through the night so I could get everything taken care of. Also, I couldn't figure out just exactly what I had to do when I got up front. The people up there were kneeling down and crying and praying, I didn't even know what to pray except the Lord's Prayer and "Now I lay me down to sleep." Somebody needed to give me some instruction, but they didn't.

It got almost to the end of the meeting, and I was afraid I wouldn't get everything settled. I still wasn't exactly sure what to pray about. Brother Wilson seemed to be preaching right at me. Finally one night there I was right on the end seat, right on the aisle. When the invitation started, no one was in my way to use as an excuse. I had to get the thing straightened out.

I don't remember exactly what I thought. It was something like, "Jesus, I don't know just what I'm supposed to do, but if you want me, I'm going up there and find out."

Right then that seemed to take care of everything. I knew just as sure as I'm writing this that Jesus was going to take care of me from then on. I felt better right then.

Up front I was told to pray. I still didn't know what to pray for 'cause as far as I was concerned it was all over with except the *thank you.* That's all I could pray about.

One of these years when you get to feeling bad and don't know why, you better remember this letter. It will keep you from hurting inside and trying to figure out a lot of things about *being saved.*

You don't have to figure it out. You just turn loose and let Jesus do it.

Memo 33: RA Tickets and a Thing

There is something about people that you need to know about and watch out that it doesn't cause you trouble. It's not something about other people that will cause them to cause you trouble. It's something that is inside of people, and you will learn it is inside of you. It's not like your stomach or your heart inside of you. It's not something physical, but it sure can cause trouble.

This probably doesn't make much sense yet. It's just 'cause this is real difficult to explain to a little kid. You had better listen real close.

Maybe I can show you what I mean be telling you what happened last night at the RA (Royal Ambassador) banquet. The R.A.s are a bunch of guys about my age. We meet once a month to study about missions and other stuff. Every summer we go to a big camp and sleep on straw inside a circus tent. We have fun except when it rains or someone throws pop bottle caps. Then we have to throw little hickory nuts back at them.

Part of my problem was that I sat at the banquet table between my RA leader and the WMU (Woman's Missionary Union) president, a woman. The other fellows all sat by each other or by their fathers. Dad was out of town, as usual. I had to sit where I did because one of the two bought my ticket or maybe both of them did. I'm not sure.

When we first started selling tickets my leader said that anyone who sold ten tickets would get one free. Well, I didn't have seventy-five cents for a ticket and I sure wasn't going to ask Mom or Dad for all of that much. I got ten tickets and at first they sold real fast. I got the tickets from the WMU president.

The last two tickets were pretty hard to sell. To tell the truth, and really telling the truth is what this is all about, I don't think I ever sold those last two tickets. Now there I go again. To tell the honest to goodness truth, I know I never sold those last two tickets.

The more I tried to sell those tickets, the harder it got to sell them. And the harder it got, the more I got to thinking how unfair it was. You see, if I sell eight tickets and some other fellow just sells two tickets, then together we have earned a free ticket. Right? Now, you know he's not going to get a free ticket 'cause no guy who has only sold two tickets deserves a free one.

But a fellow who has sold eight tickets ought to get something. After all he has earned eight tenths of seventy-five cents. With my junior high school arithmetic I figured I had sixty cents coming. So at the worst they owed me a ticket for a fifteen-cent balance, but I figured I had that much extra coming for my fine effort to sell those last two, real-hard-to-sell tickets.

Another way to look at it is that I was only trying to save food. You see, if you figure all the part tickets kids have earned but won't get cause they didn't sell all ten, that can all add up to quite a few tickets. If they cook food for all those tickets nobody gets, then they will have food with nobody showing up to eat it. You can't have food going to waste with a Depression going on like it is.

That's when this inside thing got to bothering me. Something explained it to me to turn in the money and those last two tickets to the RA leader. That's what I did. He said, "I'm sorry you don't get a free one." Just like I thought, he didn't offer to sell me one for the fifteen-cent balance.

He also said, "Are you going to the banquet tonight?"

"Sure," I told him. "It's all taken care of." It was, almost.

The WMU president lived almost on the way home from the leader's house. I almost had to go by her house, so I just stopped in to see her. That something inside just told me I ought to.

She came to the door real quick before I had a good speech all figured out about a ticket for the fifteen-cent balance. Before I knew it that something inside spoke up and said, "I sold my tickets and turned the money in to my leader. Do I get my ticket from you?"

She said, "Congratulations. Here is your ticket. Is your father coming too?"

She was disappointed that Dad was out of town. Then she invited me to sit by her. She was being nice, but I didn't want to sit by a woman at a men's and boy's banquet.

Besides that, after the thing inside me made me say that about selling those tickets, it left me standing there all by myself. To tell the truth, and that's what this is all about, when that thing inside leaves you all of a sudden you feel sort of empty and scared inside.

After getting the ticket it seemed a long time until time for the banquet. I spent some time trying to remember if my leader had a phone and could talk with the president. I didn't think he had one. I hoped not. Then, he could come walking up the street and meet her on the way to the banquet. He didn't though. I got there early to check that out, and she was already there moving the bouquet over a little because it wasn't smack dab in the middle of the table.

At last it was time to go in, but the closer I got to the door the less I figured I was going to enjoy the whole affair. It made me wonder why I bothered to sell any tickets in the first place.

One of the deacons was taking up tickets. I'd been folding and unfolding mine in my pocket for a while. My hand was mighty sweaty and the ticket looked a little sad but he took it.

"Evening, Junior. Is your dad here?"

"Nope, I ain't seen him. Could be 'cause he's out of town."

"Could be," he allowed. "Who are you sitting with?"

He was a pretty nice deacon and I thought he would ask me to eat with him if I said no one. For a minute that thing inside me said "Tell him no one dummy, and you won't have to sit with a woman."

That thing had me in a tight spot already, so I just said, "I'm settin' with the WMU president."

He said, "My, aren't you the lucky one?" He was smiling, but there was something about the way he said it—well, I don't know.

The food wasn't too good. I had to look first one way to talk to the president and then the other to talk to my leader. Then when they leaned up at the same time like they were going to talk to each other, I had to say something to one of them real fast. When you can't keep your mind on what you are eating it doesn't taste very good. Not even fried chicken and apple pie and orange drink tastes too good.

The preacher preached a home and foreign missions sermon. Then he said all us RAs should think seriously about letting the Holy Spirit lead us into being missionaries.

That thing inside me that made me not quite tell the truth wasn't the Holy Spirit. I was pretty sure of that. I was more concerned with getting out of the church basement before those two checked the money and the tickets than I was with being a missionary.

You are going to start learning to talk pretty soon. Be careful of that thing inside of you. It starts working on your tongue about that same time you learn to talk.

Dear Jr.

Alta and Billy and me did a bad thing,
I think. Do not tell Daddy. We had
ten cents and went to town after Sunday
dinner. We wanted candy and only that
one bad store was open. Alta and me
would not go in. We would not spend
money on Sunday, so we let Billy go in
and get the candy. I guess that was
all right since he is not a Christian
yet. Did we do bad? Do not tell Dad.

> *Love,*
> *P. H.*

Memo 34: Do unto Others

You are going to hear a lot about doing unto others as you would have them do to you. To most people that is known as the "Golden Rule." You have to be sure you don't do for people all the things you may want them to do for you sometime. Like keeping some guy's sack of tobacco for him, for instance.

I thought I was doing Jim a favor. Maybe I was, but it sure was no favor for me. Dad had a terrible time believing I was innocent.

Here is what happened. Jim, one of my buddies, has started smoking. He has a sack of something called Granger Rough Cut. He says it is better than Bull Durham for him.

Jim and some of the other fellows smoke after school. Sometimes they smoke in the storage sheds on the school grounds. Other times they smoke up in our favorite tree or in the big tile that goes underground behind our house.

Somebody usually has the special paper for cigarettes, so they roll their own. They don't look very good—the cigarettes that is. They're fat and the sides won't stay stuck together and the ends have to be twisted tight or the tobacco falls out. They tried using newspaper one day, but it just burnt right up and the hot tobacco fell onto the guys' legs. When they can't get the right paper now, they smoke pipes. They're real pipes they snitched from someplace.

They had to snitch the pipes 'cause the corncob pipes caught fire too. They cut cobs into short lengths and dug the pith out of the middle of them, put a cork in one end for a bottom, and stuck a cane in the side for a stem.

To try to make the cobs fireproof one guy shellacked his. That just made it burn faster and the cork caught fire too. But not until he had a puff or two. He sure puked a lot. Burnt his tongue just before he got sick. Good thing he was in the tile instead of up in the tree.

Jim wanted me to have a puff on one of his cigarettes. He says that helps you grow up faster. Dad says smoking stunts your growth. Anyway, I didn't want a smoke. Not that I'm completely against trying it, but this was too close to home.

One day after Jim had his smoke he handed me his sack of Granger. "Here, keep this for me," he said. "My old man would tamp my butt if he caught me with this."

So I took it. Then when I got home I noticed it made a pretty big bulge in my pocket. Then I got to thinking Dad would probably tamp me someplace if he caught me with a sack of tobacco in my pocket. Jim had the right idea for him when he gave me the sack, but then I didn't know who I could give it to.

The only safe place I could think of was in the old robin's nest up in the maple tree by the back porch. There was no trouble getting it up there, but then after supper I got to wondering what would happen if it rained. I climbed up and got the sack out of the nest, but my pants legs were pulled so tight with my legs around the tree I couldn't get the sack into my pocket. So I put it in the pocket of my shirt just until I could get down out of the tree.

When I got down and turned around there stood Dad. I bent over and brushed my pants so he couldn't see my shirt front. He just stood there. Next I tied my shoe, but he wasn't going anyplace in much of a hurry. So while I hunkered down there I hitched up one sock and then the other.

"What do you have in your shirt pockct?" Dad asked. His voice sounded awful loud for so far up, him standing there with his hands on his hips and me still hunkered down.

First I thought I'd say, "Did you see a hole in my pocket?" That might not have been so funny.

There were a couple more good ones popped in my mind, but I knew this was no time to get smart.

Finally I stood up and said, "You mean this tobacco of Jim's?"

"That's exactly what I mean. That tobacco, that is. Who's it is is what I'm interested in finding out."

"Well, like I said, its Jim's."

"Then what are you doing with it?" Dad wanted to know.

"Just keeping it for him."

"Why are you keeping it?" Dad wasn't going to let the matter drop.

"Well, he's afraid his ole—his father will tamp his . . . do something to him if he catches him with tobacco."

"Well now, I've caught my son with tobacco. What should I do?"

He had me there. I didn't know what he should do or was going to do, but I figured I'd better try to explain one big difference I could think of.

"Well, it's like this," I started.

"It's like what?" He just kept looking down at me. He wasn't red in the face like he sometimes got. He wasn't smiling, either.

"Well, if he gets caught with this little bitty sack of stuff, he's caught with his own. I'm not caught with my own. . . ." That wasn't coming out just right—"because I don't own any tobacco."

"All right. Give it to me. I'm going to burn this filthy stuff."

There went Jim's tobacco and he was going to be mad, but that would be tomorrow. Right then he was pretty far away and Dad was awful close.

"That's OK with me," I told him. I wasn't going to put up a fuss or he'd for sure think it was my tobacco.

"It sure hurts to think you're raising a son so stupid he gets caught with smoking tobacco to keep some other boy from getting caught."

"I was just trying to help him out."

"It's a fine way you chose to help."

"Well, you preach about being kind and helpful." I was feeling better since I could see he was beginning to let down a little.

But then he turned back on me and said, "Now don't give me any of your lip. I suppose if you saw somebody trying to shoot himself you would help him do it?"

There wasn't any use trying to explain it anymore. I just looked at the ground while thinking about things, and then I saw his feet moving off toward the house.

Jim was mad all right, but he didn't thump me. He gave his next sack of tobacco to my best friend, Earl, who was in high school and played an oboe and knew how to hide tobacco better than I did. We called him Fuzzy. He had short, blond curly hair. When you have hair like that and play an oboe you have to know how to take care of yourself.

Fuzzy and me cut an old shovel handle into short lengths and bored out a pipe bowl with his father's brace and bit. Then we put a cane in the side for a stem. Jim's tobacco didn't taste very good so we didn't smoke much. However, Fuzzy said we'd better fill the sack back up.

The problem was we didn't have any other kind of tobacco. Then we noticed that straw washed out of last year's manure on Fuzzy's Mom's dahlia bed was the same color. So we used some.

Thinking about the whole situation, what we did wasn't so much like "do unto others as you want them to do to you." It was more like Fuzzy said. "One good turn deserves another."

Memo 35: God Will Take Care of You

Dad keeps talking and preaching about how God will take care of you. I know he really believes that and I believe he is right. However, I've noticed a couple of things that go along with it. One, God expects you to do a lot to help him take care of you. The other is that you can't push your luck too far and expect God to save your neck.

Just to explain it to you, let me start by saying that Dad didn't get his paycheck on time this month. He made a trip to the associational treasurer's store in Jonesboro, but he still didn't get it.

On the first of the month and for the next two or three days Dad went to the post office early. Each day he came back walking slow and he and Mom would have a long but not very loud talk in the kitchen. Then we'd have more beans, asparagus, corn bread, and strawberry jam.

Then one morning Dad dressed up and thumbed a ride heading south. When he came back he still wasn't happy, but he had a fresh haircut so I knew he'd been to Jonesboro to see the treasurer.

You see, Dad and I have made quite a few trips over there. When we lived in Anna we'd walk over. Sometimes we'd get the check. Most of the time we'd get part of Dad's salary and hope to get the rest. Mr. Karraker would say, "I'm sorry, Brother Smith, but not enough has come in for me to pay you. I'll send it as soon as I get it."

Dad would assure him that it wasn't the treasurer's fault and we would go to the barber shop for a haircut. We'd both get hair cuts because a preacher can always use one and his boys need one at least once a month, whether he gets paid or not. When Dad got paid so did the barber. Other times he'd say, "I'm sorry, Brother Art, but Clear Creek Association is busted this month so we walked over for nothing today. Put these on my account. I'll pay you as soon as I can."

Art would say, "Don't worry about it, and maybe I can do something to give you a hand." You see, he is a deacon and knows a lot of people. He sees them often, too, with Jonesboro being the county seat.

Well, usually a few days after getting haircuts on credit we'd get Dad's check or at least part of it. Sometimes I think the barber and storekeeper may have put in a few dollars themselves. Mostly it was the barber talking to people.

Personally, I always thought if I were a barber, and shaving whiskers off the neck of some of those mossback deacons, I could have increased mission giving in Clear Creek Association.

This time something worked because Dad got a little money a day or two after going to Jonesboro. God saw to it that the asparagus and strawberries lasted until it got here.

In fact, he provided the food in the first place, but we had to go get it. Every year Dad and I cut asparagus and pick strawberries for money. We also pick green beans and sometimes Dad picks peaches and apples. When regular season is over we go to Penrod's farm and pick all we can carry home. Sometimes we get a lot more that we can carry and Mr. Penrod hauls it home for us. Then Mom cans it in mason jars with red rubber rings around their necks and zinc screw on lids.

Lately we have been eating a lot of what Mom canned. Like I

said, God will take care of you, but it seems sometimes you have to do a lot of picking, walking, hauling, and canning to help him do it.

The thing about not pressing your luck is something else. For me that means being careful around railroad freight cars.

We live close to the Illinois Central tracks. There is a side track along side the main line where they load peaches into ice boxcars. Every day the old International trucks come rattling up from the Anna ice plant several times. They are loaded with three-hundred-pound blocks of ice that are lifted up and dropped into the ends of the freight cars. That keeps the peaches good and fresh until they get to the market in Chicago, which is over three hundred miles to the north.

Sometimes we climb on the cars to see what is going on or to get ice or maybe a peach. Let me tell you, the peaches aren't good to eat. They pick them green to ship. One day we were on the box cars and a big railroad man yelled, "You kids get down offa them cars." Without even thinking, I went to the opposite side from him and jumped off.

Now if you ever want to find out how high a boxcar really is just jump off first and then look down. I can tell you its a ways down, especially if the side of the right-of-way slopes down. Well, there I was, going down fast, when I remembered "God will take care of you." The ground came up mighty quick and bent my knees double, but I didn't fall over or sprain an ankle.

The next day my legs and insides were sore. I think I was lucky that nothing got broken in that jump. I don't know how much higher that boxcar could have been and God still could have got me down OK, but I don't aim to find out.

The other way that I found out about not pushing God too far was by crawling under freight cars. We were coming home from school and there was a freight train across the crossing. Usually we crossed on the bridge, but I had to go by the post office that day. We waited and waited for the train to move, but it just sat there. We finally figured another train must be coming and the freight was waiting for the main track to clear. Anyway, we got tired of looking at the train and decided to crawl under it.

There is a lot of equipment on the bottom side of a freight car. There are lots of wheels, axles, springs, and air brake equipment. You can get down low on the ties and see a tunnel to the end of the train if the track is straight. We got to thinking about how much fun it would be to crawl the tunnel all the way to the caboose. Then we heard the train starting to move up at the front end. The engineer had backed the engine a little to get some slack so he could get started. You could hear those cars bumping the one behind them starting with the first car and coming on back.

Well, we'd seen those cars jump back several feet when the engineer does that so we figured we'd better get out from under there. The noise of those cars bumping was getting too close for comfort and I know I jumped just before the car I was under jerked backward.

The brakeman was walking along the side of the train, heading for the caboose and I popped out right in front of him. He was scared, but he didn't lose his voice.

"You kids trying to get yerself killed?" he yelled. "Don't you ever crawl under a train again. That's a mighty stupid trick." I left out some of the words he really used. It was plain to see he wasn't a Sunday School teacher.

At first I wasn't too scared. I crossed the hard road and watched the last cars and caboose go up past the depot. Those heavy wheels would go over a joint in the rails clack-clack, clack-clack. I got to wondering if they would clack or thump or thud if they went over a person. After that I felt a little queasy and my knees were a little shaky. Its just a good thing God had been taking care of me 'cause I sort of laid down on the job there for a while.

So when Dad preaches one of his sermons about God taking care of you, you had better believe him. But you better be ready to pick berries and cut asparagus to give God a hand now and then. And don't do anything real stupid or he might just figure you're too dumb to keep looking out for.

Memo 36: The Corn-smasher Rock

By the time you get into the eighth grade you will learn that some strange thoughts will come into your mind. Maybe I should say that some deep thoughts will come to mind in a strange way. It's like something you have been wondering about and can't figure out—so you put it out of your mind—suddenly pops back into your head all thought out.

Most of the time something new and different will quickly become connected to an old idea up there in your head, and then everything will be straight and clear.

I know that sounds confusing, but maybe if I tell you a story it will make sense.

In Sunday School the teachers talk about the Bible being the Word of God. They say it is part of our heritage. It has been handed down to us by all people who have been gone a long time. The Bible is supposed to be like something precious that's been in the family a long time, like some of Grandma's old antique dishes. We're supposed to keep them nice because they are old and she can't give us any more like them.

Most Bibles that kids get aren't old. They are new Bibles we get for Christmas, birthdays, or in time to practice for Sword Drill contests. It's hard to imagine them as heirlooms handed down from old times.

After Dad has used a Bible for a few years it sure looks old, but it's no antique. It's just a worn-out Bible that's been used to death, and it would not make a very good hand-me-down. It has too many notes, underlines, and dirty pages from his studying. Slapping it on the pulpit hasn't helped it much either. Putting it under his arm instead of on his head when it rains has helped some. He says that "God's Word mustn't get wet." But that didn't keep his Bible from falling into the baptistry once.

Anyway, I've been having trouble understanding about brand new birthday Bibles being handed down from old historic characters. It seems more like they have come from printers and clerks at the book store.

The thing that got me to thinking straight was something that came to mind the other day when I was climbing around in some bluffs east of town. The bluffs are tremendously high limestone rocks that have straight up and down faces. You climb part of a hill to get to them and there is usually a lot of hill on top of the bluff. When you are standing on top of the bluff you are higher than the tops of the trees growing at the bottom of the bluff.

Some bluffs can be climbed. Some have ledges and cracks, and caves go back into some. My favorite bluff has a cave with a ledge in front of it. It is high up so that I can look south for miles and miles. The cave is like an apartment and the ledge is like a front porch.

I was sitting on the ledge the other day wondering if old John, the last Indian around here, really lived in the bluffs like some people say he did. I was just looking and lazying and dreaming and wondering about the round patch of dirt on the ledge.

The dirt was smooth and fine. It appeared to have washed into a hollow spot in the rock and settled firm when the water dried. Then I wondered how deep it was. With a stick it was easy to poke down to the hard rock bottom. I started digging out the dirt and found that the hole was just like a great big mixing bowl. Then I uncovered a rock in the middle of the bowl.

The rock was a little bigger than my fist. It had a big knob on the bottom and a smaller knob on top. I'd seen pictures of rocks like that before. It was a smasher rock used to crack corn or other grain that had been placed into the bowl-shaped place in the ledge.

That rock really got me to thinking. Some Indian had mashed corn right there on that ledge. Then he had left the smasher right there and dirt had washed into the bowl and hidden it.

I slowly put my hand down over the top knob. I wondered who was the last human to have held that rock the same way and how long ago it had been. Some person had left his smasher rock right there just for me.

But then I thought it wasn't really his rock. It was God's rock. He made it. The Indian just used it for a while. Maybe others before him had used it for years. And it was God's bluff too. Only he could make a beautiful, majestic limestone bluff. Why, the whole world was God's. He made it all.

Then I thought about the Bible. It is God's Word. He began telling things to man after he made the world. Man just wrote down what God revealed to him over a long, long period of time. Men put God's Word into their own words just like some Indian put God's rock into something he knew how to use.

I guess then I understood more about the Bible being God's Word and handed down from generation to generation. What's handed down is not the copy of a book. It's the word that's inside a book's cover.

That corn smasher is a precious rock. I wonder about it a lot and we use it to hold the front door open. Come to think of it, God's Word holds open a pretty big door, too, the door to heaven.

VI.   High School and Later

"When you pull a pendulum so far to one side, you must remember that it swings just that far the other way when you turn it loose. You need to remember that, David." Those wise words were spoken to me by my high school English teacher, Elsie Yehling.

She was reminding me how far a preacher's kid is pulled aside from the rest of the world by parents and some church people. It was her opinion that when I got away from home and church I would try to swing into a wild life-style. She knew that at least there would be a great temptation to do so. I've thought of her kind words many times.

During my teen years and until I went into the Army, other teachers, church members, friends, and relatives taught me many lessons. Some things are learned the hard way, but kind people soften many of the blows.

I hope my last few memos to P. H. saved him at least a few moments of grief.

Memo 37: I Haven't Been Called

Trying to decide what kind of work you want to do for a living is serious business. I don't mean the work you have to do to earn a dollar while growing up. It's the lifetime work you choose to do to earn your living after you've grown up that's so hard to choose. I want to tell you how it is now so you can get a head start on your thinking about it.

My big problem is that so many people think I should be a preacher. Mom and Dad talk a lot about Uncle Henry being a preacher, Dad being a preacher, and how many of the Wards and other ancestors were preachers. They stop just short of saying, "And you should be a preacher too."

The unusual thing is that Dad preaches and talks about God calling people to special service. However, neither God nor anybody else has called me for anything. I've sat through revivals, the missionary appeals at RA camp, and listened to the returned missionaries, but nothing has ever made me feel that's what I should do.

I keep thinking, *Lord, I'll do what you want me to do.* Then nothing very spectacular happens. Not that I expect to get hit over the head or anything. There's just nothing. I even think a lot about the still-small-voice approach. There's nothing coming in on that circuit either—not even when you are sleeping and I'm laying awake thinking about it.

Sometimes just to keep me thinking about it, Mom says she would like for one of her kids to be a doctor or nurse. That doesn't stir me up much, either. Cutting on people and giving them big pills or sticky syrups wouldn't be much fun.

In the meantime, I find other work to do while going to school. I'm the church janitor and I can repair radios. Maybe I'm suppose to work at what is available. That way the Lord can make available what he wants me to do and I'll do it.

The principal at high school is a wonderful man. He has talked to me about a vocation. He has asked about my being a preacher. He understands about it being a calling rather than something I choose. Then he said some things that really made me think.

He said, "David, you see firsthand what a minister should do, and what your father does well. That should be helpful to you if you do become a minister."

I had to agree with him on that. Then he went on talking.

"You also see mistakes that he makes, don't you?"

"Yes." I had to admit that Dad had done some things that members thought were wrong. I had some doubts about his being right about them also.

"That can help you two ways," Mr. Reid said. "If you become a minister, you will know some things you shouldn't do. Some mistakes you shouldn't make."

"I think I see what you mean," I told him.

"But look at something else," he continued. "I'll bet you see some things that need to be done in a church that someone other than your Dad can do best. What about the business side of church work? What about buying things for the church or arranging for repairs on the building or doing the treasurer's work? If those things are done right by a member of the church, doesn't it save your Dad a lot of worry?"

"Yes, it sure does."

"Well, maybe you should think about doing something like that to save ministers or missionaries from having to do things that interfere with what God called them to do. You know, it just could be that you are supposed to earn your living at something other than preaching, so you can use the insights you gain as a preacher's son to greater advantage."

Now, I had to admit he might have something there. I hadn't even thought along that line before. Since he started my thinking that way, I've considered what he had to say in connection with my spare-time jobs.

Sometimes I get a radio to repair. I'm not too good at it yet. Most of the time it's just a tube burned out. The regular repairman in Elkville sold me his used tube tester for $6.00. Now I can find a lot of the troubles. He sells me tubes wholesale so I can make a few dollars on them. In return I take him the difficult jobs so he can make some money from them. It works out pretty good for both of us. And you know what? Churches have sound systems in them that need installing and fixing. Also, we have the Baptist Hour on radio. There may be a job there for a preacher's kid.

The church janitor's job isn't much fun. I don't care for sweeping, waxing, and dusting. In cold weather the old furnace has to be kept going. I bank the fire, but sometimes it goes out and a new fire has to be built. Carrying in coal and carrying out ashes is hard work.

I've noticed, though, that when the church is warm and clean, everybody seems happier and things go better. This makes Dad happier and his job easier. Maybe there is something other than preaching for me to do to help make things better for those God does call.

Memo 38: The Light on the Steeple

Ringing the church bell is the best part of the janitor's job. It's fun to ring it any time, but the first bell on Sunday morning is the one that pleases me most. There must be many people still asleep at that time. Waking them up is a special pleasure.

In fact, I enjoyed ringing the bell so much last Sunday that I turned the bell over. That was when I learned about the electrical wiring for the light on the front of the steeple.

In case you have never seen a church bell, they are rotated on an axle just like a big wheel. In fact, a big wheel with a grooved rim around it is mounted on the same axle alongside the bell. The pull rope goes up one side of the wheel, lays in the groove and goes up and over the top edge of the rim. It goes down the opposite side and is fastened to the bottom of the rim with a clamp or may be just tied to the rim.

The rope is supposed to be pulled only enough to give the bell a big loud ring. If you pull too hard, that bell, which is almost balanced but a little heavier open-end down, will flop right over. Then there you are with a rope over only a small part of the wheel or completely out of the groove. To put it all back in position, someone has to climb up into the steeple, grab the rim firmly, and flop the bell over. The rope has to be placed back onto the rim. It could be done by pulling the rope up into the steeple and lifting it over the bell. The trouble with that is the knot on the end of the pull rope. It's too big to pull up through the hole in the vestibule ceiling. Its easier to turn the bell over than to untie the knot and pull up the rope.

The whole town knows you goofed when you turn the bell over. When it goes back over it clangs once or twice and that's all. It seems to say, "Ding dong, he did it again."

Anyway, I turned the bell over, got the ladder, and climbed into the steeple. That bell is dirty. So is the steeple. The sparrows and pigeons see to that. Only the preacher's kids find themselves in that kind of a mess on Sunday morning, and with their good pants and white shirts on.

I got the bell over. Believe me, in the steeple next to the bell is no place to be when it clangs. When it went back over I jumped back and almost stepped into the electrical wiring going to the steeple outside light. Now, I'm not much of an electrician, but something about that wiring didn't look right.

I cleaned up after climbing down. The ringing of the second bell was done very cautiously. Sunday School started on time. All during class that light wiring kept coming to mind.

During hymn time of the worship service I was busy in the choir. By the time Dad had got far enough into the sermon for me to know I'd heard it before, that wiring began to make sense. About halfway through the sermon, I thought I had it figured out. By the time we stood up to sing the invitation hymn, I couldn't help looking at the trustees one at a time, wondering which one had wired the steeple light.

As soon as the congregation had gone I turned on that light. The little wheel that turns in the light meter when something is using electricity never moved. Just to make sure, I turned on the inside lights and sure enough the meter started working.

Someone had wired that outside light ahead of the meter. Sometimes people do this in the attic of their home to cheat the power company. However, this is the first time I've heard of a church doing a thing like that. And now the big problem is what to do about it. I'm not about to tackle the rewiring job. The power can't be turned off where those connections have been made.

I suppose the best thing to do is to quietly tell one of the trustees who is more friendly to me than the others. Perhaps he'll take care of it. If it is up to me to tell him, Dad is never going to find out. And its surely something that should not be brought up in business meeting.

Some things that you will learn about churches, little brother, you will wish you had never found out.

Memo 39: The Bank Fund

Playing a trombone in the high school band is a lot of fun. Playing on the football team is also enjoyable. But with the band practicing marching, and all the football practice we have, I see more of the football field than I really care to.

It's rather difficult to be in the band and on the football team. The band plays at the halftime of the ball games. I can't march with them while dressed in the football suit. Besides, the coach is talking to us about all the mistakes we made during the first half of the game. So I practice all that marching for nothing.

When we get back out of the dressing room after the halftime, we have to wait for the band to finish and get off the field. There they are in uniform coats and clean white pants. And there I stand in a dirty football suit with my hair all messed up. Some of the band members sort of turn up their noses at the team. The sousaphone player doesn't, though. He knows he'll get dirt clods tossed into his horn if he smarts off.

When the band gives a concert the football team gives me a bad time too. They say things like, "Don't throw a pass at the clarinet player," or "Don't blow that thing too hard without your kidney pads on."

The big trouble comes from the band director and the coach. They both want their share of my time. One gives me a grade in music. The other gives me grades in physical education and math. It's tough trying to keep them both happy and get good grades.

I really had a problem because I tried to help the band finances. Our director told us we needed more money for music, instruments, and travel expenses. He also said that the band budget was as big as it could be. If we got more money, we'd have to give another concert or think up something else.

After giving the situation a lot of thought it finally occurred to me that when people bought a ticket to the ball game they got to see and hear the band too. So why shouldn't the band get a share of the gate receipts from the ball games?

I made the proposal to the student council which seemed to think it wasn't too bad an idea. The principal tried to sit back and pretend the students could decide what to do. The coach yelled bloody murder and said, "Who the h___ dreamed up that stupid idea?"

Things were bad enough right then, but they got worse immediately 'cause someone told him it was my idea. So guess who didn't get to go to Carbondale with the football team the next week? I had to practice all week then was told not to bother making the trip. The band wasn't going, so that was out too. The only thing left was to hire the school bus at Mr. Frederick's standard price and sell enough rides to pay for my ticket and make a few bucks for myself. I got there, but I didn't enjoy the game very much.

Well, the upshot of it all was that the band didn't get any of the ball game money. I got a good grade in music and a fair grade in math. The math grade would have been worse but the principal made the coach refigure it.

Maybe the coach had a point. One day he said, "Do they take up an offering at your church to pay your dad?"

"Yep, they do."

"Well, how'd you like for them to take part of it to pay the choir first and then give him what is left?"

Now anyone who knows our choir knows it would be stupid to pay us anything the way we sing. But then the coach hasn't heard us. I don't think he goes to church.

So I just said, "I see your point."

I must have said it just right 'cause next he said, "You'd better suit up for the next game if you think you can lay off of the athletic fund."

My advice to you is to play basketball and sing in the quartet. And don't worry where the money comes from.

Memo 40: Personality

In one of the classes at school we were discussing personality. Someone mentioned split personalities and the discussion became very lively. Some students believed a person could have a split personality, and others felt very strongly that it just couldn't happen. I kept very quiet because in my opinion it would be easy for a preacher's kid to have two personalities. But I wasn't about to try to explain it all to the class.

It seems difficult for me to determine what I do just because I am me, a person, and what I do because I am the son of a preacher and am expected to do certain things just because Dad is a minister. Most of the time it would be more fun, or maybe the phrase is *more natural,* to just live and react as an individual. However, there is always a feeling, an awareness or almost consciousness, of having to react in a manner determined by those who are constantly observing. It's sort of like being on stage. Actors must have difficulty telling when they are acting or really living.

It appears that actors at times live their roles. At other times it seems that they are acting when they should be living their real life. It's about the same way with preacher's children.

For instance, how many high school freshmen are Sunday School teachers? You can bet the pastor's oldest son will be, and it is likely that his other sons will be also. So pay attention in your class. You will probably be teaching those same lessons very soon.

Now the teaching isn't difficult. The class is a group of lively Junior boys. I love them and we have a good time while studying.

They look up to a high schooler so other than wiggling and shoving each other they generally behave.

But I have to ask myself if I'd teach that class if it were left entirely up to me. The rest of my gang is in a class with a man for a teacher. Here I am teaching and expected to set an example just because I'm a Sunday School teacher.

In some members' opinion the example that has to be set is not one of a normal, moral teenager. It is more like a young person acting like an adult is supposed to act. Some of those adults don't set such a good example either, but that's no excuse for the preacher's kid to kick up his heels. Just trying to act like an old man will make an old man out of you.

Another situation in which I would just like to be myself is at the store where I work part-time. There I have to react as the public expects Brother Smith's boy to react. However, most of those people who come into the store don't act like Brother Smith expects church members to act.

The other day a customer came in and walked right up to me and asked, "Are you the ____ order boy?"

I had delivered the afternoon grocery orders a couple of hours earlier. There was no order for him so I wondered what he was so red-faced about.

"Yes, I deliver the groceries."

"Well, why in the ____ didn't you deliver mine?" He shoved his face right up into mine. He'd been drinking.

"I'm sorry, I didn't have an order for you." By then my face was getting pretty red too.

"The ____ you didn't. My wife said she called it in to you. You callin' my wife a liar. I'll have your __ for that."

Of course, you know we don't talk like that at our house. In fact, that is the first time in my life that anyone has ever directed that kind of language toward me.

My memory is a little hazy about some of the things that occurred next. I recall that suddenly the man's whole expression changed. From red anger his face went to white fear. Then I remember the butcher saying, "It's all right, Smitty," and he took a can of peaches out of my hand and put them on the shelf.

What had happened was that the man's wife had called in an order. Another clerk took it and forgot to give it to me. When the man started handing out the verbal abuse I was his innocent victim, and I almost planted that can of peaches between his eyes. That was one time when a normal reaction would not have been as appropriate as the preacher's kid's expected behavior.

So now when the going gets rough, I just detach myself from the situation and observe instead of participate. When I have it all figured out, or know pretty well what behavior or corrective action is most appropriate, then I react. That's OK, but it sure puts a strain on your own natural impulses.

On the other hand, it does have some advantages. It keeps a person from making mistakes by flying off the handle. Also, the pause to take a second look or thought seems to be developing into my natural reaction. Maybe I'm developing a more grown-up personality to replace my younger one.

The last personality thing I want to tell you about has to do with playing ball. That is a game one should be able to play by being his natural self. You would think a person should be able to throw, bat, and catch without having to think too much about it. Not so for a PK.

We were playing Elkville Methodists the other evening. They don't have much of a team so we were beating them pretty bad. In fact we had scored so many runs that the game was still going rather late in the evening and there were no lights.

I was pitching and even the other team knows I'm not a fast ball pitcher. In the last half of the last inning, with the Methodists trying hard to catch up, you'd have thought the old ball was really blazing in there. The Elkville team and spectators were all yelling, "Play fair" and "Throw 'em easier."

Some of the crowd really got on me. "A preacher's kid wouldn't take advantage of the dark like that." Someone even yelled, "Remember the Golden Rule." Of course you try not to pay attention to things like that, but they do get to you to some degree. They cause you to start thinking about how you are acting instead of just being your natural self.

At first I decided to pay no attention and just play the game. Then I thought, "Maybe I'm not being fair and should let up a little. Finally, it came to me that they were just trying to take advantage of my being a PK. They were just trying any way possible to win the game. That last thought really did it, so I just zipped the ball in as fast as I could, and we got that final inning over in a hurry.

That may seem like a lot of words. It may appear to be unrelated to personality, but I don't think so. From what I've learned so far, most people struggle with being two people—the one they are and the one they want to be.

Paul had something to say about doing the things he didn't want to do and not doing the things he wanted to do. PKs have to add that other diminsion—trying to be the person that the church congregation (and a whole batch of additional people) wants them to be.

Your personality will probably be a blend of all three of these. The trick is to get them all molded together and not let them tear you apart. Only the good Lord can help you with that.

Memo 41: The Furnace Grates

If you ever get to be the church janitor just pray that the building is heated by a gas or oil furnace. Our building has an old coal fired furnace in the basement. There is one large grille directly over the furnace and in the floor near the front of the sanctuary. The cold air return is down the basement stairway at the back of the auditorium. It's not a very efficient system, and it takes a lot of work to keep it operating.

The church does not have a coal shed and there is no coal bin in the basement. So the coal is just piled out back of the building. One of the members hauls it in a horse-drawn wagon. Wet coal is not very good for starting fires. Snow and ice make it difficult to get coal from the pile. When the coal is in large lumps, which it usually is, it is great for banking the fire, but small pieces for starting fires have to be obtained by breaking the big lumps with a hammer.

Kindling is any old board that someone doesn't want. Mostly it's scrap lumber from the mines. Mostly it has knots or nails that make it hard to split.

We have an ugly old pile of ashes too. I've made paths, drives, and covered the parking lot with ashes and still they pile up. All those ashes have to be carried up the basement steps. Not all the ashes get carried out that way. The cold air ducts are in the bottom of the furnace on both sides by the ash box door. No matter how carefully I move the ashes from the furnace a heavy dust goes into the cold air ducts, up through the jacket around the furnace, and through the heating grille. Then it settles on the pulpit, piano, and pews from where it must be removed with a dust rag.

The furnace is very old but it usually works well if the grates are in good shape. The grates are made of cast iron. They are like heavy grilles and are between the fire box and the ash pit. The fire lays on top of the grates. Air comes into the bottom of the furnace and up through the grates to the fire. Ashes can pile up in the pit and shut off air for the fire.

The grates have gears on one end and when one grate is moved all of them move. A rod from one grate extends through the furnace and the shaker handle fastens onto it. Sometimes those grates don't want to move, making it difficult to shake the ashes down.

Also the grates sometimes break or get bent. Then they won't shake at all. A few weeks ago the grates broke in two. That made it more difficult to operate the furnace, but the bad thing about it was that the trustees thought it was my fault for shaking the grates too hard.

It took a long time to find new grates. A furnace repairman from DuQuoin finally got them by ordering them from some foundry. The furnace worked very well with the new grates. It was much easier to shake down the ashes, and because the new grates didn't sag down into the ashes, they were much easier to remove.

I should have known that things were going too good to last. Big trouble soon came my way.

You see, if there are no services from Sunday night to Wednesday night I have to make a decision. Either I bank the furnace and give it some attention every day or let the fire go out and build a new fire late Wednesday afternoon. If the weather is very cold it is better to bank the fire and have a little heat in the building. That is what I did a couple of weeks after the new grates were installed.

On Wednesday when I started to fire up again, those grates were in sad shape. They had sagged onto the ashes. When I removed the ashes and tried to move the grates with a poker they stuck to the poker. That cast iron actually pulled out in long strings like taffy candy. I didn't feel so good stooped over looking at that mess.

I told Dad about the grates and he told one of the trustees. Soon there was a committee meeting in front of the furnace. Boy, they sure asked a lot of questions.

Some of them thought I had let the ashes pile up too high. I don't know for sure. Maybe I didn't take them out often enough.

Someone else said that didn't make any difference; that good grates shouldn't melt and sag like that. Someone suggested that the grates had been newly cast and were still green, whatever that is. Anyway, the same furnace man had to get more new grates and put them in for half price.

If the janitor had been someone other than the preacher's son, it would have been rough. But when one of the deacons said, "Guess we'd better fire the preacher and get us one with a boy who knows how to take care of a furnace," I got pretty shook up. He was looking at a trustee and smiling and winking. That didn't keep me from worrying about Dad losing his job. Annual business meeting won't come again for several months, but some deacons have a long memory.

So you just remember if you get to be janitor; keep the ash box clean, don't shake the grates too hard, and most of all, don't goof up before the annual business meeting.

The following note was placed under a note that Dad left for me. You can guess what Dad's note said.

Dear Jr.
I am sorry you were bad and went to
see that girl after Dad said not to.
It is too bad you have to build the
fire in the morning. Please shake
the stove quiet and do not make a lot
of noise with the coal bucket and
please sleep on the cot in the front
room. I do not want to wake up that
early.

P. H.

Memo 42: My First Tailored Suit

Today should have been a happy day, but somehow it wasn't. For several weeks I've looked forward to wearing my new tailored suit. Finally it arrived; a dark green pinstripe that fits perfectly. But sitting up there in the choir while Dad was preaching, I noticed how shiny the back of his coat and the seat of his pants are. Somehow it would have been more appropriate for him to have the suit. He wouldn't want it that way, of course, but it would have made me more comfortable.

There is some story behind that suit, though. I'm out of high school now and working full time at Bradley Supply Company. Full time means sixty hours a week at twenty cents per hour. I'm a clerk and delivery truck driver.

Mr. Bradley owns the store. Many people think the coal mine

company owns it because the store gets money from customers who are miners by having it taken out of their paychecks at the mines. Mr. Bradley has to pay the mining company to make the wage check off and the customers have to agree to it.

This arrangement makes it possible for miners to buy many things on time payments. Of course Mr. Bradley adds a percentage to the time pay plans, but where else can you buy everything from motor oil to men's suits for a dollar down and so much per payday?

We always enjoy the days that the suit salesman spends at the store. About twice a year he comes to town in his big black car. He has a chauffeur and the back seat and trunk of his car are full of pictures, patterns, and material samples. The salesman's name is John. He is always smiling and joking.

John and the chauffeur carry in the patterns and samples and drape material all over the dry goods part of the store. Word gets around, so soon the men begin coming in one or two at a time and before you know it John is measuring the first customer.

It's an education to watch John work and kid the fellows into buying a more expensive suit than they first planned on. He measures chests for vests that fit snug. Stomachs get measured and jabbed and compared to chest sizes. If a fellow's waist is bigger than his chest old John practically puts him on a diet and cinches up the waist like he expects the guy to lose a few pounds before the suit is delivered.

I didn't know that shoulders came in so many sizes and shapes. John showed me all different kinds of stoops and slouches he has to allow for. It appears the coal miners shovel a lot and develop strong shoulders. But they also work in tunnels, which make them stoop. That's why they buy tailored suits instead of ready-made. At least John convinces them that is the reason for buying tailor-made.

Pant leg length is a big problem. Some want them long, some short. Again, if the waist is bigger around than the inseam is long John tightens the belt line. He even checks the side the fly opens from.

There is one part of the whole process that keeps taking longer and longer. With each sale, right after the measurements are taken, John and Mr. Bradley take the customer across the street to the tavern and buy him a drink. By evening on a busy day the last suit takes a long time for John to measure and the celebration lasts until after closing time. I'm surprised that the last suit fits, but it always does.

About a month after John's visit, the suits begin coming in. Some men bring their wives with them and change clothes in the feed room. Then they come out all dolled up and parade in front of the wavy old mirror up in front of the store. Mr. Bradley walks around and looks, and the guy's wife does the same. They always agree its a great suit, a good buy. The check-off system always takes a little off the paycheck until the suit is paid for.

The last time John came to town he seemed very glad to see me. I helped him carry in samples and noticed he had some very nice material. I never dreamed I could ever afford one of those suits.

After he was all set up to sell suits, John called me over. He looked at Mr. Bradley and said, "Dan, Smitty here would sure look good in one of my suits. Why don't you give him a good deal and let me measure him up?"

Old Dan pushed his hat back on his head and scratched his bald spot. "Well, now he does work pretty steady. He ought to stick around long enough to pay for it at a couple of dollars a week. Tell you what I'll do. I'll let him have it at cost if you give it to him less your commission."

"It's a deal," John said as he whipped his tape measure from around his neck. "You let me pick the pattern and cloth, Son, and I'll fix you up a suit like you never had before."

What'll it cost," I gulped.

"Never mind. You can afford one of John's suits. Hold still while I check this inseam again."

I can tell you John knew more about my anatomy than the family doctor before he finished. He allowed how I was on the skinny side, but would grow a little more and fill out some. He said I was slightly bow legged, but I think he was being kind; I couldn't see what he wrote on the order blank. And he said he better allow a little more in the shoulders 'cause he could tell since his last visit that lifting one hundred pound bags of feed was developing me there.

Old John spun me around so many times I was almost dizzy, but not as unsteady as his older customers after their trips across the street. And I was beginning to worry about that celebration because I wasn't going over to the tavern with them. Besides, John knew my dad was a preacher.

When he had finished, John stood back and took one last look at me from top to toes. "You'll look great, Smitty. Just wait till you see what I've done for you."

Turning to Mr. Bradley he said, "He's too young for drinking, Dan, what'll we do to celebrate his new suit."

"How about a soft drink on me?" I asked.

"Don't mind if I do. Better for me than that cheap beer, anyhow."

So we had a soft drink and I asked again, "How much will that suit cost me, John?"

"How does twenty-four bucks sound to you?"

That made me do some fast figuring. It would take twelve weeks to pay for that suit. Ten dollars pay instead of twelve. Take out for Social Security, a dollar twenty for tithe, and five for Mom for room, board, and laundry and there wouldn't be much left for savings or goofing around.

"Sounds OK," I replied.

"That's a fifty dollar suit, Smitty. You'll be proud to wear it."

So that is how I came to get a tailored suit. When it finally came in, I wouldn't go to the feed room to try it on. I brought it home and the whole family stood around while Mom and I took it out of the box.

At first I wondered about the color. Dark green with a little blue tinge to it wasn't one of my favorites. Mom said to try it on before making up my mind about the color. That made the difference. All you kids said there was enough blue in the green to almost match my eyes, which I had always thought were just blue—still do.

Anyway, inside the coat on the pocket it said "Tailored expressly for DHS" in gold lettering. That made me feel pretty proud. Dad said it was sure a good suit. And, like I said, I'd liked for him to have had a new tailored suit, too, but he couldn't climb into the pulpit with a green pin stripe instead of his blue serge. It wouldn't look right, and those coal miner deacons would accuse him of drinking beer with Dan and John. I wonder if any of them wear one of John's suits.

Memo 43: Our First Family Car

You sure are getting a kick out of riding in our first car. You sit in the middle of the front seat astraddle the gear shift lever with your nose almost touching the windshield. Dad and you and I sit up front. Mom and Dad don't know how to drive so it appears that I'm the family chauffeur until you get big enough to take over.

Mom and the girls fill up the back seat and away we go. Since we have always had to borrow rides in someone else's car, we are finding it a pleasure to go where we want to go and when we want to go. We have had some family picnics, and we went to Nashville to see Grandpa just because we can now get away when we want to.

The car is a 1929 Model A Ford so it is over ten years old. I'm buying it from Uncle George who has the Chevrolet garage over in Christopher. You may have to decide about buying a car someday so I'll tell you how all of this came about.

I lost my job at Bradley's. At first that seemed very bad because I was working a year so I could save enough to start to college. But it appears that everything will work out better.

Our family never did buy groceries from Bradley's. I think that kind of bothered the old man. Then one of his good customers got after Dan to hire his boy. Finally, so much was said about our not trading there and the other family being so deserving, Mr. Bradley said he would have to let me go.

I noticed he didn't do it before I got the suit paid for. Maybe I should have bought two suits.

Anyway, he said he'd write a letter of recommendation for me and he wrote a good letter too. Now I'm selling Fuller brushes.

At first I just sold here in Dowell, where I could walk. Sales were good and it was evident that I'd need a car to get to other towns. Carbondale is in my territory and with it being the biggest town I'll have to spend most of my time there. I was beginning to want a car pretty bad, so I just hitchhiked over to Uncle George's to see what I could work out with him.

He asked me how much I had for a down payment. I didn't want to take all the money out of my bank account so I said I had twenty dollars. He asked me about the brush sales and about my territory. Then he said, "Let's go out on the lot and look around."

We walked right past the shiny ones up on the front of the lot and all the way to the back row of cars near the fence. Uncle George looked at a couple of them, and I kicked a few tires just like I knew what I was doing. Then he looked under the hood of this Model A and opened the doors for a look inside. He got in and turned the key, stepped on the starter, and what do you know—it started.

He left it running and got out. "Want to try it out?" he asked. I climbed in and eased the car out of the lot and drove around the town for a few blocks. It didn't look like a limousine, but the best I could tell it ran pretty good.

Back at the garage I pulled onto the lot but didn't back up to the rear where the Model A had been parked. Uncle George is a good salesman so he noticed that.

"Gonna take it, eh?" he chuckled. "It's a four-door sedan. Be easy for Grace and the kids to get in and out of."

I realize now that Uncle George knew more than I about what this car was going to mean to his sister and her family.

"How much do you want for it?" I asked.

"How about sixty bucks?"

Right away I knew I would take it at that price. Then I thought I'd try to dicker him down a little. But I knew I'd have to arrange payments, and it didn't seem right to haggle with an uncle. Finally I just asked, "How do you want me to pay the forty?"

"I'll leave that up to you. You pay me as much as you can when you can, but try to pay something every month."

"I'll do it."

"I know you will, Junior. Come on in the office and we'll have my secretary fix up the papers for title and license."

With that done we went back outside, shook hands, and I started to leave, then I got an idea. "I thought you always filled the gas tank when you sold a car," I suggested.

"We do when we sell a new one."

"Well, it's new to me."

"You're as big a tightwad as your grandpa," Uncle George growled, but he was grinning. "Back up to that pump, and I'll put five in it. That ought to get you home."

So that's how I bought the car. And that sure started a lot of other things happening.

Suddenly I have more friends, but not many of them buy gas for the car. Only Richard does that. He and I have been friends for a long time. His dad has a Model A. He also has a repair manual so Richard and I have overhauled the motor of my car (as you could tell from the parts that were scattered over the backyard).

Some of the neighbors and church members were betting we wouldn't get it back together correctly.

You will be interested in a simple way we made one of the repairs. The body of the car slid to one side at the rear. It almost touched the top of the left rear wheel. Richard and I tried to jack it back into place but couldn't get the body brace to slide across the rear spring, which goes across the back from one side to the other.

We fixed it by going to the strip mines and placing a big rock on the right side where we had removed a rear seat cushion. I drove over a rough road until the body jolted back in place.

Then Richard yelled, "Hold it." He then dropped the center bolt through its hole in the frame and rear spring. I stopped and we put the nut on the center bolt, threw out the rock, and put the back seat in place again. Job done.

The best thing about having the car is covering more territory to sell Fuller brushes. The more places I can go, the more prospective customers I can contact and the more sales I can make. Sales are good and with forty cents of each dollar as profit I have been making a lot more than Dad does. This causes a problem, especially when I don't work hard all day to earn it.

You may not know it, but Dad makes twenty-five dollars per week. Well, I try to sell twenty dollars worth of merchandise a day. If I do I get eight dollars. This makes forty dollars a week, less travel and lunch expense. Some days that is hard to make and then other days I go way over it.

Like the other day, the third house I went to I sold a twenty-four dollar order. By noon I'd made about three day's wages. It was a hot day so I came back to Dowell, found Richard, and we went swimming at the strip mines. Dad found out about that 'cause somebody saw me go by Richard's house. He thought I should have kept on working, but the way I see it I'd already made as much as he was going to make all week so I had a swim coming.

Either I have to keep working or get Dad interested in swimming. But you can be sure if he ever did, some deacon would say he should have been visiting or studying on a new sermon.

By now I think the best thing about the car is that it gets me out of town away from the church members. That plus the extra money is almost as good as not having to worry about deacons, trustees, and annual business meetings.

By the way, the car is almost paid for. I think Uncle George is sizing me up for one of those shiny ones on the front row of his lot.

Memo 44: A New Garage

This is my first memo to you since we moved to Pinckneyville. Dad is pastor at Oak Grove, three miles north of town on the state highway. We have traded cars because Dad has to cover more territory as the church members are in town and scattered all over the country north of town. Our little '37 Willys is sort of small for a family our size, but it runs good and doesn't use much gas.

Dad and I are splitting the payments on this car. My Model A was the down payment. I drive to Carbondale to college five days each week. Classes take the morning and selling brushes and driving home takes most of the afternoon. Saturdays are for delivering brushes and taking Dad visiting. I don't know which is the busiest, me or the Willys.

About the only time we have trouble with the car is early mornings when it is snowing or sleeting. We needed a garage. By now you know we have a new one. What you don't know is how I got into big trouble with Dad over that garage.

We had been talking about how much we needed the garage, but Dad hadn't done anthing about it. You see we rent from Brother Keene, a respected longtime Baptist and member of the First Baptist Church. He is a nice old gentleman. I like him, but in my opinion he is tight with his money. Dad likes him and in my opinion is a little afraid to cross him.

Mom kept trying to talk Dad into pressuring Brother Keene about the garage. He said he'd mentioned it once and had been turned down. We had a few more cold days when the windshield was frozen over with ice. The car wouldn't start. I was late for classes. Then Mom talked impatiently at breakfast. That was before you kids got up so you didn't hear her.

Dad got all red in the face and said, "All right, Grace. We won't talk about it any more." So we all shut up.

A few days later it was cold again, and I said something to Mom about needing that garage. She said, "If we get a garage, Son, you are going to have to take it on yourself to get it."

That was all I needed to get going. A day or two later I walked into Brother Keene's office. "Hello. What can I do for you, David?" He looked a little surprised to see me.

I sat down and politely as I could said, "You could build us a garage."

Brother Keene's eyebrows were kind of scraggly and they went up very fast. He just looked at me for a long time. I just sat still and kept my mouth shut.

At last he said, "I think this is something your father should discuss with me, don't you?"

"No, I don't," I replied, still trying to be calm and courteous while looking him right in the eye. If he was a pillar in the church, and as good as his reputation, he sure wasn't going to throw me out.

"Why not?" he asked.

"Because he already has asked you and you refused. But we still need that garage. Dad's work and mine are suffering because we have car trouble because we have to leave our automobile out in the open. He just gets worked up and aggravated but won't cross you because he's afraid of what trouble you can cause him at his church and in the association."

"I see," Brother Keene said. Then he leaned back in his swivel chair and looked straight at me. I wasn't selling brushes that afternoon and he had a warm comfortable office. I just stared back and kept still.

It seemed like a lot of time went by. Brother Keene finally leaned forward and in a very even voice said, "We'll see what we can do."

I stood up, shook his hand and said, "Thank you, Sir." Then I got out of there. A day or two later a carpenter showed up and started on our new garage. It's not very fancy but it keeps the rain and snow off of the Willys.

Dad stopped by to thank Brother Keene for fixing him a garage after telling him no. Brother Keene let the cat out of the bag by saying, "That oldest boy of yours is quite a lad, Brother Hosea."

Of course, Dad wanted to know why he said that and Brother Keene told him. For a few days he didn't say anything to me about it. In fact, he was pretty quiet around me and looked like his feelings had been hurt—which I guess they had. Maybe it was pride more than just feelings.

One night after the rest of the family had gone to bed, Dad and I were in the kitchen reading. All he said was, "Son, I wish you would let me take care of the family business from now on."

The way he said it I didn't feel very smart alecky. "I'll try not to interfere again," I promised. I didn't interfere, but as it turned out I had to take care of a lot of family business.

Memo 45: Dad's Heart Attack

For a few days you have been a frightened little boy. You and the girls have all been very good about keeping quiet and letting Dad get plenty of rest and sleep. All of us have felt very strange because we are not used to seeing Dad in bed all the time.

Maybe if I tell you exactly what happened you will understand and not worry too much. It happened this way. Len and Betsy Schmidt were visiting with us. Usually they go home rather early. However, that night they stayed a little later than usual. I think now that they may have noticed Dad wasn't feeling just right. They stayed until after you kids had gone upstairs and to bed.

Dad was sitting in the little rocking chair that Grandma Smith uses when she is here. As we talked he kept rocking slower and slower. He began to look a little pale to me. He began to lick his lips every once in a while.

Then he quit rocking and gave Mom a very wide-eyed look. "I'm not feeling very good, Grace. I think I'd better lie down," he said as he started to go to the couch. He didn't make it. Brother Schmidt and I caught him as he started to sink to the floor. We laid him on the couch. He was white as a sheet and not breathing much at all.

We called Doc Hiller. It seemed like it took him a long time to get to our house, but it was really just a few minutes. All the time, Dad just laid there very still, turning whiter.

Doc took just one quick listen with his stethoscope while reaching into his bag for a hypodermic needle. All in one motion he loaded the needle and stuck it in Dad's arm. Then he listened and listened, but it seemed to me that nothing happened at all. Neither Doc nor Dad moved. The house was very quiet and still as we all stood around and watched. Mom wasn't crying, but she had her hands clasped very tightly together.

Soon Doc reloaded his needle and gave Dad another shot. He kept bent over and listening for several more minutes. Then he began to sit up straighter in his chair and smiled at Mom just a little. "He's beginning to come around now, Mrs. Smith. Nip and tuck there for a bit."

Slowly Dad wasn't quite so grayish white. Then he began to look a pale pink, then pink. He took a few slow deep breaths and blinked his eyes. Next he opened his eyes and looked up at all of us looking down at him.

"Good morning," Doc said. "Enjoy your nap, preacher? Keep that up and your deacons will get you for sleeping on the job."

Dad tried to smile, and in a weak voice asked, "What happened?"

"You tried to cash in your chips on us," Doc told him. "You've let yourself get into a pretty weak condition, Preacher. Your old ticker can't take any more of that. You're going to have to take it easy for a while and get a few things off your mind."

Doc had us carry Dad into the bedroom. Mom and Doc got him into bed, then Doc gave him a shot to put him to sleep. He left a lot of pills and instructions for Mom. Then he left. As he headed for the door he said, "I'll see you first thing in the morning. Call me any time tonight if you need me, but I think he'll be OK."

Mom and I didn't talk much after the Schmidts left. I slept downstairs on the cot. Mom stayed with Dad and he slept like a log all night.

So we have all been quiet for several days, and Dad is doing better. He started to worry the first day or two then he found out Oak Grove was going to keep paying him while he was off sick.

Two days after Dad's heart attack, Lloyd from the Kroger store came knocking on the door and asked if I wanted a full-time job as a clerk. I took it. We needed the extra money for doctor bills, better food for Dad, and some of the other things Dad had been worrying about. I couldn't be going to college in Carbondale every day with Mom needing me close to home.

Dad didn't like it at first when I quit school. He cried a little and said it was all his fault. I told him it wasn't either. He wore himself down taking care of the Lord's work. The Lord had provided me a good job just when we needed it so he could get well again.

I have a lot of years for going to school if I want but not much time with Dad if he doesn't get some help.

You and the girls have been very good. I've threatened you a few times if you try anything 'cause Dad can't lay a hand on you. No trouble from you yet. Even the girls have quit quarreling over who gets the bobby pins for her hair at night.

Doc Hiller spends a lot of time at our house just joshing with Dad. Of course Dad fusses at him about giving him so much attention. Doc just says, "I'm only loafing and saving my strength, Preacher, like you ought to do more often."

Now that's the way it happened. Dad is going to be all right. We're going to have plenty to eat, and I'll see that you get some new school clothes. So smile once in a while, and don't look so scared.

Memo 46: So Long, Little PK

It is getting late tonight. You and the rest of the family are asleep. I have been very quietly packing some clothes so that I can leave early in the morning. As I look over at you there is a sly smile on your face. Wonder what you are dreaming about?

This is my last memo to you. You are growing up OK, and I'm leaving in the morning to go into the Army Signal Corps. Please forgive me for sneaking out, but I'm no good at good-byes. They hurt too much sometimes.

Mom wanted to get up and fix breakfast early for everyone. When I asked her to just let me take off early while its still dark and get a quick bite at the restaurant, she agreed. She and Dad understand how it is.

Don't worry about Dad's health. He is doing all right. Doc says he may not be good as new but that he is good for a long time. You just keep the kindling cut, the coal buckets filled, and the ashes carried out. Keep him from getting aggravated at a lot of little things. See that he remembers to have the car greased and oil changed on schedule.

Mom will need you to run more errands than you are used to doing. You'll have to take care of the mail I used to take to the post office on the way to work. And you'll probably have to stop by the store on your way from school to get the things I used to carry home after work.

I'll be back early next spring. Marge and I plan to get married then. Don't pay any attention to any gossip you hear out around the church about our having to get married. If that were the case we wouldn't be waiting until spring. I'll just get to come home one week-end for a physical exam and another for the wedding. That will be enough to start the tongues wagging. I can hear them now saying, "My, that sure was a hurry-up affair."

Don't worry about how you're going to get along without my being around to help you when you are in trouble. You are a Christian now. Just remember that the Lord will look after you, even taking care of a lot of little things you won't even think of.

You grew up quite a bit when you flattened Cecil last week. You slugged him just like I told you to. Some bigger guys have to be handled that way. You are probably wondering about a Christian doing something like that. Look up some Scriptures about righteous indignation. They may not be absolutely appropriate in your situation, but they will make you feel better.

I still haven't been called for preaching or missionary work or anything like that. Maybe my calling was just to buy a car for a preacher's family and to drive him around in it so he could get his visiting done. Maybe looking after the family until he got well was just part of my calling. Anyway, it appears that the army will get me overseas quicker than the Foreign Mission Board usually does.

One last thing I want you to know. There will be times when you doubt that you are a Christian and that there is anything to this whole church and preaching thing. I haven't lived much longer than you have, but let me tell you that I can see how it all works out for the good in the long run.

Just remember that if the devil can make you doubt and confuse you enough, you won't do anything for the Lord. I'm going to have to think about that a lot myself. Let's both try to remember what Paul said about all things working together for good for those who love God and are called according to his purpose.

So long, little PK.

Love,

Junior

Postscript

Dear Junior:

I have just returned from a visit with Mother. We had our usual review of where all her children are and what we are doing. Rereading some of your old memos to me caused a lot of conversation.

It seemed significant to us that God has used each of us in a unique way. Betty, Marjorie, and Alta have stayed in their communities to serve a local church. Monta spent years in Alaska as a kind of advance home missionary.

I was a foreign and then a home missionary while in the Marines. Now I'm in one of the locations here in California that has been identified by the Home Mission Board as having a great need for evangelism. And you have given almost thirty years to the establishing and developing of new churches in Peoria, Joliet, and Chicago, Illinois.

Surely God prepared each of us for the special work only he could have known we were to do.

We also talked about the wonderful people of Clear Creek Association. After so many years they remembered Mom and Dad's years of hardship during the Depression, and called Dad again as associational missionary. Then they built the new house the folks got to live in for almost ten years until Dad retired. They meant so much to all of us when Dad had another heart attack and passed away.

I hadn't heard from Bill Hickem in a long time. He is now the associative executive secretary of the Florida Baptist Convention. I remember my note to you which you left with the memos. I recall our buying candy on Sunday and having Billy make the purchase. Actually, Alta and I were not Christians at that time. We just thought we were because Dad preached.

Bill says that incident caused him to realize clearly that he was unsaved. It was one of the things that led to his acceptance of Christ as his Savior.

God does work in mysterious ways. May he continue to bless you. Keep writing.

Love,
P. H.